But If Not...

Mastering the Art of Letting Go

Ronald Higdon

But If Not...

Mastering the Art of Letting Go

Ronald Higdon

Parson's Porch
Books
Cleveland, TN

Parson's Porch Books

Copyright (C) 2011 by Ronald Higdon

ISBN: Softcover   978-1-936912-26-1

All rights reserved. No part of this book may be reproduced or transmitted in any form or by any means, electronic or mechanical, including photocopying, recording, or by any information storage and retrieval system, without permission in writing from the publisher.

This book was printed in the United States of America.

To order additional copies of this book, contact:

Parson's Porch Books
1-423-475-7308
www.parsonsporch.com

Acknowledgments

As the years increase, so does my gratitude and appreciation for the many congregations where I have been privileged to pitch my tent on my sojourn of faith and ministry. I only wish that the resources I have found through family systems, the Center for Congregational Health, and the Alban Institute had been mine to share with the earlier congregations. I am not the same person or minister I was when I first assumed pastoral responsibilities. However, this is always the way life – even the life of faith – works. We can only be who we are and where we are. I'm grateful I'm not still there.

Colleagues and friends continue to enrich my life and contribute greatly to my ongoing development both personally and professionally. Their encouragement and support have led to this second publishing endeavor.

This book is dedicated to my two sons, Mark and Michael. They have continued to exhibit the qualities of integrity and hard work, doing what they believe they are called to do regardless of how it turns out. Their high principles and ethical behavior continue to convince me that my wife and I must have done something right! We certainly don't take credit for their achievements but recognize they have come a long way in mastering the art of letting go as I have tried to describe it in this book.

Table of Contents

Introduction   **11**

Part I: Reality 101

Three Little Words That Make for a Disturbing Story: **17**

     "But If Not"

     (Daniel 3:13-18)

Who Designed This Prayer Book?   **31**

     (Psalm 22:1-11)

Who Started the Rumor That Christianity Is Easy?   **45**

     (Matthew 10:34-39; John 6:66-68)

Points to Ponder   **64**

Part II: Responsibility, Not Results

You Are Among the Called   **66**

     (Ephesians 4:1-6)

Who Am I That I Should Do It?   **79**

     (Exodus 3:9-12)

Doing Some Simple Thing   **94**

     (II Kings 5:10-14)

Points to Ponder   **107**

Part III: The Bottom Line: Relationships

What is God Up To? **108**
    (II Corinthians 5:19)

Nicodemus Isn't the Only One
    Who Doesn't Understand **125**
    (John 3:1-10)

A Wrestling Match We All Face **138**
    (Genesis 32:22-30)

Points to Ponder **151**

Part IV: Action! Action! Action!

Christianity is a Way of Life **153**
    (Ephesians 4:17-24)

Right Here! Right Now! **166**
    (Matthew 24:45-51)

Not Perfection, But Maturity **177**
    (Matthew 5:43-48)

Points to Ponder **188**

Part V: On Being Inner-Directed

The Amazing Power at Work in Us   **191**

   (Ephesians 3:16-21)

Have You Heard Any Good Silence Lately?   **205**

   (II Kings 19:9b-13)

Who's Holding the Cue Cards?   **217**

   (Luke 7:31-35; Matthew 5:34-45)

Points to Ponder   **228**

Conclusion: The Real Secret   **230**

Bibliography of Quoted Sources   **241**

About the Author   **249**

INTRODUCTION

It may be the most arresting statement about spirituality I have ever read: "All great spirituality is somehow about letting go. Trust me on this crucial point."[1] I want to pair that with a recently found observation from someone in another tradition: "I have found joy in letting go of what I think I want and doing what is in front of me. To do what we are doing completely, and then to drop it just as completely and go on to the next activity when it is time – that's our practice."[2] After years of study, conversation, workshops, prayer, and much reflection, I have come to believe that these observations are right on target. This is the theme we will be exploring in this book.

Whenever someone tells me, "I think there are some control issues here," my response is usually, "Control is THE issue." The reason we don't want to let go is because we refuse to relinquish keeping our hands on some desired outcome. Recognizing that most of the longed for outcomes are beyond our control remains difficult for me to this very day. I have learned the hard way (in spite of the fact that we can learn in other ways) that when despair is the final reason for letting go, we have paid a much higher price for that decision than would have been necessary had it been done earlier.

Although technically not a sequel, after completing *From Fear to Faith: The Spiritual Journey From Anxiety to Trust,* I was convinced that mastering the art of letting go is absolutely essential to that journey. One of my wife's favorite questions is, "Could you unpack that?" I will attempt to do just that by looking at sixteen biblical texts with theological themes that relate to practical matters in the life of faith. As was true of my previous book, no theological degree or advanced biblical knowledge is required for understanding this material. It is often forgotten that Paul's letters in the New Testament were written for the "average" Christian in the first century. His gospel message was not for a select few elites or full-time church leaders. Almost always, he wrote to people who already had full-time lives but needed to know in what specific ways their new faith related to everything they did and everyone they met in their ordinary work-a-day world.

The ancient Chinese curse, "May you live in interesting times," probably needs several strong additional adjectives even to begin to hint at the chaos and uncertainties of our time. "Deconstruction" is one of the words often used to describe postmodernism, even though Jacques Derrida (who gets credit for it) did not actually use the word.

A joke that made the rounds during the years when the *Godfather* movies created a mystique for the Italian

Mafia, summed up all the primal fear and fascination that America's learned elites had toward the Derridean phenomenon. Question: "What happens when you meet a deconstructionist in a dark alley?" Answer: "He offers you a deal you can't understand."[3]

My purpose is two-fold: (1) to present understandable and doable biblical insights for our time (insights that enable us to function a little more effectively with purpose, hope, shalom, and joy – as biblically defined), and (2) to encourage personal reflection and conversation. To make some progress in this direction (the only really achievable goal in spiritual development), we will examine the reality of living in a not yet fully redeemed creation, the basic calling that belongs to all Christians, the essential elements in the Kingdom of God, the need for practice as well as belief, how we discover what we ought to be doing, and where our work ends with the surrendering to God the things that only God can do and trusting him with the future (the final consummation).

There are five major divisions in the book; each chapter concludes with "Reflections," and each division is followed by "Points to Ponder." These "points" are intended to assist in your personal reflections and to provide starters for group discussions. We begin in the Introduction with an Old Testament story that presents the theme for the book. Part I addresses the harsh realities of troubles faced by those who attempt to do right. Part II discusses "calling" as belonging to all Christians and not restricted to vocations in ministry. Part III maintains that the Kingdom of God has to do with reconciliation and relationships. Part IV is a reminder that doing (action) is literally the way we live out our faith (i.e.: *faith without works is dead* – James 2:17). Part V deals with how and where we get our directives for living. The conclusion uses a recent best-seller, *The Secret,* to underscore a basic biblical teaching that ought to be twittered everywhere.

In the Bibliography of Quoted Sources you will find a wide variety of references. I have never felt it necessary to endorse everything in a book in order to receive valuable information or genuine wisdom. Restricting life choices to "safe" selections that only reinforce what one already believes has never seemed to me to be the way of spiritual and intellectual growth. Opposing ideas can not only promote dialogue but also challenge me to reexamine my points of view. This does not mean I am constantly changing what I believe; it does mean that I keep alive at the center of my faith and do not shift into the defensive mode of "Don't confuse me with any other way of looking at things." This seems to me to be the problem the Scribes and Pharisees had with Jesus.

As always, nothing I have written is intended to be the final word. It reflects where I am and my understanding after years of continuing to be a beginner in the faith. From another writer comes my philosophy: I hope you will find much in this book that is helpful and encouraging. Whatever else you find, simply let it fall from your hands like so much sand sifting through your fingers. Your responses and suggestions would be appreciated. Information about the author, including an email address, will be found at the back of the book.

Unless otherwise indicated, scripture passages are taken from the New Revised Standard Version.

---

[1] Richard Rohr, *The Naked Now* (New York, Crossroad Publishing, 2009), 64.
[2] Norman Fischer, quoted in Patrick Henry, *Benedict's Dharma* (New York, Riverhead Books, 2001), 89.
[3] Carl Raschke, *The Next Reformation* (Grand Rapids, Baker Academic, 2004), 13.

Part I: Reality 101
Chapter 1: Three Little Words That Make for a Disturbing Story: "But If Not"

MODERN OBSERVATIONS:

One always commits oneself before fully knowing what one is committing to. There is no such thing as a commitment that is made only after all the evidence is in. Commitment is based not on facts, but on desire – the root meaning of desire is to follow a star.[1]

"I've learned that you can tell a lot about a person by the way he or she handles these three things: a rainy day, lost luggage, and tangled Christmas tree lights."
-Maya Angelou.[2]

"Shedding regret for the past and concern for the future, you will begin to live fully in the present moment, which is the closest thing on earth to eternity."
-David Yount.[3]

But If Not...

THE BIBLICAL TEXT: Daniel 3:13-18; NRSV:

> Then Nebuchadnezzar in furious rage commanded that Shadrach, Meshach, and Abednego be brought in; so they brought those men before the king. Nebuchadnezzar said to them, "Is it true, O Shadrach, Meshach, and Abednego, that you do not serve my gods and you do not worship the gold statue that I have set up? Now if you are ready when you hear the sound of the horn, pipe, lyre, trigon, harp, drum, and entire musical ensemble to fall down and worship the statue that I have made, well and good. But if you do not worship, you shall immediately be thrown into a furnace of blazing fire, and who is the god that will deliver you out of my hands?"
>
> Shadrach, Meshach, and Abednego answered the king. "O Nebuchadnezzar, we have no need to present a defense to you in this matter. If our God whom we serve is able to deliver us from the furnace of blazing fire and out of your hand, O king, let him deliver us. But if not, be it known to you, O king, that we will not serve your gods and we will not worship the golden statue that you have set."

Required Rethinking

I suppose it was understandable that I did it then; to do it now would be inexcusable. As a boy in Sunday School, the story from Daniel 3 was one of my favorite biblical stories. It was with childhood delight I imagined the great trick the three Hebrew young men were about to play on the king. My tragic mistake was that I brought the end of the story into the middle of the story. My reading of the text required no real courage or faith on the part of the three because, in my stories, the heroes always won and the villains always got their due and right always won the day.

I had no idea what it means to face those in power who are *in furious rage*. With these words the writer describes the king before whom our three heroes are summoned. Literally the text reads *in rage and hot wrath*. I had no idea of how dangerous it can be when one decides to do what one is convinced is right.

In my "love of adventure" mind, I compared Shadrach, Meshach, Abednego, and Daniel to Indiana Jones and Luke Skywalker. In doing so, I reduced the lions Daniel faced to house cats and the fiery furnace to a sauna. There never was any real danger, risk, or peril. Now I know better. The four in the cast from the book of Daniel are Hebrew captives in Babylon. An eating contest related in chapter two elevates the four to places of leadership in the kingdom but by chapter three we meet the inevitable. Some of the Babylonians resent having these foreigners exercising authority over them and they plot to eliminate them. They do so by reporting to the king that Shadrach, Meshach, and Abednego are not participating in the civil religion as the king has commanded.

Advance Decisions

Nebuchadnezzar can hardly believe what he is hearing. He calls in the three and asks, "Is it true? Is this a joke? Are you serious?" They reply, "It is true. It is no joke. We are serious." The king responds, "I'm serious too. *If you do not worship, you shall immediately be thrown into a furnace of blazing fire, and who is the god that will deliver you out of my hands?*" Three little words spoken in reply to the king's threat summarize with shocking simplicity the nature of their faith-stance. "We do not doubt the ability of our God to deliver us from your burning wrath, but that is not the issue. We don't presume on the power or purposes of God. He may save us, BUT IF NOT it really doesn't change a thing. We will not serve your gods or worship the golden statue you have set up."

"We have no need to present a defense to you in this matter," is the announcement that this has been an issue long settled in the minds of the three. They do not have to wait until the golden statue is built or until they are summoned before the king to make up their minds about what they will do. Some things came with the territory of their identity as Hebrews.

What the king erects is quite impressive and what he

asks doesn't seem too extreme. The statue is ninety feet high and nine feet across. It is a wooden structure overlaid with gold and bears the image of the king's favorite god; it is covered with inscriptions. All the king asks is that with the announcement from the musical instruments, everyone join in a time of communal worship. Most have no problem adding another god to the others they already worship. Shadrach, Meshach, and Abednego worship the God whose demand is singular and who forbids the making of graven images. They know who they are and whose they are. This means a lot of questions are settled before they ever come up.

    If you live with everything up for grabs, then a lot of things will grab you. If you settle the big issues in advance, many things will be strictly "no contest." Jess Lair suggests that far too many people have reversed what he calls the law of the universe: they move from having to doing to being. First, they decide what they want to have; then they decide what they have to do to get it; then they are convinced they will be somebody. Lair contends the law of the universe flows in the opposite direction: from being to doing to having. You begin by deciding who you are. Out of that discovery and the gifts you have naturally emerges what you will do. After that, what you have takes care of itself.

    I believe this is exactly what happens in our story. "But if not" reflects the *a priori* identity decision. What they tell the king is: "We know what we must do...regardless of how things turn out." The focus is where it ought to be: on actions and not on results. The first question in faith (and life) is always: "What ought I to do?" The first question is not: "What will happen to me?" This is what the art of letting go is all about; it is all about input, not about outcome. It's all about walking by faith, not by sight. An honest question at this point is: "Can this bizarre tale possibly be a story for the 21st century?" My answer: Not only possible, but absolutely necessary. The time in which we live needs a powerful story like this one from the book of Daniel. The need is underscored for me by two items. The first is from *The Speed of Trust* published in 2006:

> *Consider the percentage of students who acknowledge that they cheated in order to improve their odds of getting into graduate school: Liberal arts students – 43%; Education students – 52%; Medical students – 63%; Law students – 63%; Business Students – 75%. (Author's comment): "How does it make you feel to know that there's more than a 50% chance that the doctor who's going to perform surgery on you cheated in school?"*[4]

The second item is a tongue-in-cheek list titled "Realistic Proposed Revisions of Our Favorite Hymns." Here is the list:[5]

I Surrender Some

Oh, How I Like Jesus
I Love to Talk About Telling the Story
Amazing Grace! How Interesting the Sound
Spirit of the Living God, Fall Somewhere Near Me
Take My Life and Let Me Be
Just As I Pretend To Be
O for a Couple of Tongues to Sing
My Hope is Built on Nothing Much
I'm Fairly Certain that My Redeemer Lives
My Faith Looks Around For Thee
Blessed Hunch
Pillow of Ages, Fluffed for Me

In a revisionist world, Shadrach, Meshach, and Abednego never looked better and never had more to say to us than in their declaration, "But if not…." Making advance decisions does not mean we never change our minds or positions on anything. It means we have a basic understanding of what shapes our identity, where our loyalties and commitments lie, and what boundaries we will not cross.

Living With Risk

The temptation is to read a story like the one in Daniel 3 and assume that God always intervenes on behalf of those committed to doing the right and the good. The biblical narrative hardly gets underway before we have a denial of this premise. For reasons not given, Cain finds both himself and his offering unacceptable to God; his brother Abel is presented as the model of being right and doing right. *So Cain was very angry, and his countenance fell* (Genesis 4:5). After God's warning about the danger of his attitude, in the very next verse, Cain kills his brother. The shocking lesson early in the pages of scripture is that doing right, being good (however else you want to phrase it) does not necessarily "pay off." "But if not" may turn out to be exactly that. There is not a single recorded word from Abel; he disappears as quickly as he appears. The only thing we know about him is that *the Lord had regard for Abel and his offering* (Genesis 4:4) but does not see fit to reward him with protection.

The great host of unnamed heroes in the roll call of faith in Hebrews 11, ends with a huge declaration of "not" (11:36-37):

> *Others suffered mocking and flogging, and even chains and imprisonment. They were stoned to death, they were sawn in two, they were killed by the sword; they went about in skins of sheep and goats, destitute, persecuted, tormented – of whom the world was not worthy. They wandered in deserts and mountains, and in caves and holes in the ground.*

The three Hebrew children refuse to presume on the

will and purposes of God. Often there is a high price to pay for taking the high road, for standing for justice (always the definition of God's righteousness in the Old Testament), for living as Kingdom citizens (as described in Matthew 5-7 in the Sermon on the Mount).

We always take a risk when we love our enemies by doing good to them and praying for them. Although Jesus' explicit command (Matthew 5:44), it is no guarantee that our enemies will become our friends or even moderate in their attacks. We do it because we are living by another standard; we are people called to be the salt of the earth and the light of the world (Matthew 5:13-14).

Settling some questions in advance does not mean we are assured of the outcome; it means we know where we stand. In 1961, a *The Charlotte Observer* newspaper carried a story about Carlyle Marney. Here is an excerpt from that article:

> In 1961 Carlyle Marney hired an African American, a Johnson C. Smith graduate, for his manuscript typing. Marney said, "She's a good secretary. It did cause some concern, but from outside my church more than from within. Someone once asked me what I would do when an African American presented himself for membership in our church. (I replied that) I will do two things. I will say, 'As of right now, I am this man's

pastor.' Second, we will meet in two weeks to decide whether I am his pastor and your (the congregation's) pastor, or just his pastor."

Something Always Happens

There is, of course, the rest of our story and my thesis: whatever the outcome there is something that always happens. In this story, the king has the three thrown into the furnace. When he looks in to see them in their misery, he announces in amazement: *I see four men unbound, walking in the middle of the fire, and they are not hurt; the fourth has the appearance of a god"* (Daniel 3:25). Whether an angel or the Lord himself, the figure is a God-given presence. Here is the one certainty among all the uncertainties when one does what is right.

When the king looks in, he sees three plus one. This story is all about the plus one. *But if not...*means that God steps into the furnace with us. Psalm 23 declares: *Even though I walk through a valley as dark as death itself, I will fear no evil, FOR YOU ARE WITH ME* (emphasis mine). This is THE promise with which the Gospel of Matthew begins and ends: *...they shall name him Emmanuel, which means "God is with us"* (1:23); *"And remember, I am with you always, to the end of the age"* (28:20). Hebrews 13:5b-6 echoes the same promise: *...for he has said, "I will never leave you or forsake you." So we can say with confidence, "The Lord is my helper; I will not be afraid. What can anyone do to me?"*

But If Not...

There is something else that always happens. It is reflected in the classic line spoken by John Wayne in the movie *The Alamo:* "There is right and there's wrong. You've got to do one or the other. You do the one and you're living. You do the other and you may be walking around, but in reality you're dead." This will be treated later, but the fact not to be ignored is that "we become what we do." What does this mean for the three heroes in our story? Someone shared this with me: What is important is not the fire in the furnace but the fire in the bones of the three; the image was ninety feet tall but they were nine hundred feet tall; the image was just overlaid with gold – they were solid gold; they stood head and shoulders above the powerful king. They could do right in the face of his threats – with no guarantee.

We've heard so much about the pleasures of doing your own thing, going your own way, looking out for number one, etc. that we have forgotten the privilege and joy of doing your duty, assuming your responsibility, doing what is right. In the psalms, the writers continually speak about the joy of doing God's will, of obeying God's laws. I think we have forgotten just how alive you feel, how good you feel, when you know you have done what is right, what is good, what is just.

Reflections

The stance of faith exhibited by the three Hebrew children is not very often reflected in current popular theology or preaching. To say "However it turns out, I stick by my decision," is to live without guaranteed outcome. "Tithe and the Lord will give it back to you ten-fold" is a message without biblical foundation. *"Bring the whole tithe into the storehouse, that there may be food in my house. Test me in this," says the Lord Almighty, "and see if I will not throw open the floodgates of heaven and pour out so much blessing that you will not have room enough for it"*(Malachi 3:10) is Scripture. Interpreting this text is not quite so simple. The promised blessings may have nothing to do with material goods; they may be blessings recognized only by those who have eyes of faith! Malachi 3:10 is not the formula for winning heaven's lottery!

The assumption persists (perhaps because it is so widely and popularly proclaimed) that it is possible to live a charmed life: if you trust enough, if you believe enough, if you pray enough, if you read your Bible enough (and sometimes, if you support the right ministry!). I can't find any evidence that this world has ever offered a charmed life to anyone – religious or not.

Only the week before writing this, I had a conversation with a business owner who described the depression one of his employees was battling because her prayers were not being answered. Her local pastor as well as her "TV pastor" assured her that God was in the blessing business and her job was simply to "name it and claim it." She kept naming it and claiming it but she never got it. I never learned if this woman's depression resulted from her disappointment with God or with herself or simply with life in general.

Philip Yancey provides this relevant comment:

> *When I began writing about my faith, I concluded that I had only one thing to offer: honesty. I had heard enough church propaganda growing up. I would cling to the stand of a pilgrim, not a propagandist, describing life with God as it usually plays out, not as it is supposed to play out. Not everyone agrees. A publisher once asked me to consider changing a book title from DISAPPOINTMENT WITH GOD to something cheerier, perhaps OVERCOMING DISAPPOINTMENT WITH GOD. I thought about it, decided to keep the title, because disappointed people were the ones I wanted to address*.[6]

Harry Emerson Fosdick once said: "To feel that God is not living up to his good reputation is one of the most poignant, inescapable experience the saints ever face."

The problem almost always has to do with anticipated results. There is no disappointment if we have decided to live with "whatever happens" and rest on the assurance that God is faithful and will never forsake us – however things turn out.

[1] Patrick Henry, *Benedict's Dharma*, 8.
[2] Quoted in Susan Sparks, *Laugh Your Way to Grace* (Woodstock, Skylight Paths, 2010), xvi.
[3] Quoted in Brent Bill, *Imagination & Spirit* (Richmond, Indiana, Friends United Press, 2002), 185.
[4] Stephen Covey, *The Speed of Trust* (New York, Free Press, 2006), 12.
[5] *The Anglican Digest,* (Eureka Springs, AR, 1999), Easter.
[6] Philip Yancey, *Soul Survivor* (New York, Doubleday, 2003), 270.

Chapter 2: Who Designed This Prayer Book?

MODERN OBSERVATIONS:

> (The psalms are) messy and disordered, like life….At a basic level, the psalms help me reconcile what I believe about life with what I actually encounter in life.[1]

> Strange and powerful sections of the Bible, rather than being candidates for ridicule, are opportunities for insight. Such possibilities may not unfold to the casual reader and indeed there are things that take a lifetime to understand.[2]

> I have always struggled to get past the baffling inconsistencies of the Psalms.[3]

THE BIBLICAL TEXT: Psalm 22:1-11; *The New International Version*:

> *My God, my God why have you forsaken me? Why are you so far from saving me, so far from my words of groaning? My God, I cry out by day, but you do not answer, by night, but I find no rest. Yet you are enthroned as the Holy One; you are the praise of Israel. In you our ancestors put their trust; they trusted and you delivered them. They cried to you and were saved; in you they trusted and were not disappointed.*
>
> *But I am a worm, not a human being; I am scorned by everyone, despised by the people. All who see me mock me; they hurl insults, shaking their heads. "He trusts in the Lord," they say, "let the Lord rescue him. Let him deliver him, since he delights in him."*
>
> *Yet you brought me out of the womb; you made me feel secure on my mother's breast. From birth I was cast on you; from my mother's womb you have been my God. Do not be far from me, for trouble is near and there is no one to help.*

Good Questions

Both the title of the book and, in particular, one of the chapter titles intrigued me. The book is titled *Who's Afraid of the Old Testament God?*[4] (My silent answer was: "Just about everybody who's read all of it!"). The last chapter in the book is titled "What Kind of Prayers Would You Publish If You Were God?" (and under my breath I said, "Certainly not all of those contained in the book of Psalms!").

Along with those two questions and my two quick responses, I remembered two things that are so easily forgotten. What we call the Old Testament (the Hebrew Bible) was Jesus' Bible; it was what he heard and read as inspired Scripture. What we call the book of Psalms was Jesus' prayer book and hymn book. And there is plenty of biblical evidence that he knew his Bible well and he joined the other faithful in praying ALL the prayers in his prayer book.

Many of the psalms with their violence, call for unbelievable cruel vengeance against enemies, and downright despair have caused much concern in the Christian community. Also disturbing are those complaints about God being inactive, asleep, or just nowhere around when he is needed.

Psalm 22 is one of those upsetting psalms, even more so when we note its usage by the Gospel writers in the Passion narratives. Mark notes the dividing of Jesus' garments and the people deriding him and wagging their heads as referenced in Psalm 22:18 (Mark 15:24). Matthew (27:43) uses Psalm 22:8 when the people say, "He trusts in God; let God deliver him now."

Much concern (with numerous attempts to alter its harshness) has come from 15:34 in Mark (the earliest of the Gospels) and the words the Gospel writer gives as Jesus' last words from the cross – his final prayer: *My God, my God, why have you forsaken me?* (Psalm 22:1). In a book of "Famous Last Words" we certainly don't expect this to be the memorable quote at the end of Jesus' earthly life. But it is. Directly from Jesus' prayer book.

A Good Prayer Book

In spite of (or because of) the messiness and disorderliness of the psalms, two positive assessments can be made. First, Psalms is an excellent prayer book; it was for Jesus, and it is for us. It is a good prayer book because it forces us to deal with the full spectrum of life and faith; it calls us to honesty.

During my pastoral ministry, I recall visiting a woman in her eighties who was having a pretty tough time. As I entered the room, I gave my usual opening question, "How are things going?" Her response was, "Better now. A while ago, I had a visit from Ms. Sunshine and it takes a little time to get over it." I never knew the identity of Ms. Sunshine, but I understood what was meant. The trouble with Ms.

Sunshine was that she made no connection with the pain and suffering of the person she was visiting. My rule of thumb in hospital visitation: let the patient set the agenda for the conversation.

A true story may best serve to illustrate the reason for such negative reactions to the Ms. Sunshines of this world. A minister writes about his conversation with a woman who came to see him because of her deep depression. The depression was understandable because she had just received a rather grim medical diagnosis. She asked if the minister could suggest any spiritual reading that might help her as she struggled with God's mercy and her own mortality. The minister suggested that she read through the one hundred and fifty psalms, ideally in one sitting but over not more than two or three days, that she read them without commentary, in an unfamiliar English translation, and that when she finished she come to see him again.

She did as he suggested and when she returned, the minister asked how it had gone. Her response was that she had been amazed by the range of emotion and intensity in the psalms. "Whoever wrote them," she said, "had exactly my same sense of ups and downs, exaltation and despair." The minister writes: "She felt secure in knowing that somebody else had had the same set of roller-coaster emotions, and that it was all right to feel anger, joy, consolation, frustration, peace, turmoil, and resignation, often at the same time, for they were the emotions of the psalmist and they gave her permission to respond to God and to her circumstances just as the psalmist did."[5]

Richard Foster expresses it clearly: "The psalms teach us to pray our inner conflicts and contradictions." My question is: where did we ever get the idea that we shouldn't pray what we really feel? I contend this is our real prayer, whether we verbalize it or not. The psalms encourage us (and enable us) to verbalize it.

If we don't get things out on the table, how can we deal with them? How can God's Spirit help us deal with them? And I mean, get EVERYTHING out on the table. When you pray, don't hold back! Let the psalms be your model for "letting it rip." I did a sermon once I titled "Nice Prayers Finish Last." The thesis for this reasoning was that most of these prayers are not real prayers. They do not reach to the depth of our souls. They do not touch the deep pain, despair, and doubt that lurk in the dark shadows.

Faith Stretching

Praying the psalms also helps us face the real questions and issues of life and faith. Like the one presented in the front page article titled "I-65 Crash 'Stretching' Man's Faith" in the Louisville *Courier-Journal* of March 26, 2011. The article referenced the accident in March 2010 when a tractor-trailer crossed a median, tore through a cable barrier, and collided with a van carrying the Esh family and friends to a wedding. In that accident, Amos Esh lost his parents, three sisters, a brother, sister-in-law, infant nephew, and two family friends.

The article quotes Amos: "Sometimes you're very strong in faith and very OK with what happened. Other times you wonder why it happened or why it had to happen this way....It has been very faith stretching." To which the writers of the psalms would shout, "Amen!"

"Faith stretching" may be a gross understatement. For too many, episodes like this can become faith destroying. It is tragedy beyond belief. It is tragedy beyond all reasonableness. What we boast of as "The American Dream" has given us many things. Unfortunately, it has not provided us with a strategy or philosophy for dealing with tragedy and calamity and devastation. Most Americans, at best, have an inadequate theology of suffering; many don't have any.

Simply voicing how tough calamities are to handle and how much they challenge our faith is very therapeutic. Psalm 130 begins with the plaintiff: *Out of the depths I cry to you, O Lord.* This is one of the group of psalms known as the Psalms of Lament – and there are over 50 of them. Martin E Marty goes so far as to rate half the psalms as "wintry."[6] And most of these psalms are largely ignored! They seem to be superfluous to the multitude of Sunday assembled saints who gather to hear only good news and blessings. They make little room for those who have struggled all week to find anything other than blessings so mixed that it is difficult to sift out any good news.

Eugene Peterson admits that only a minority of the psalms focus on praise and thanksgiving; perhaps as many as seventy percent take the form of laments.[7] Walter Brueggemann has coined the term "psalms of disorientation" to describe those psalms that express confusion, confession, and doubt.[8] Phillip Yancey in *The Bible Jesus Read* (a book I highly recommend) has these observations on the book of psalms:

> *People around me used the book as a spiritual medicine cabinet – "If you feel depressed, read Psalm 37; if your health fails, try Psalm 121" – an approach that never worked for me. With uncanny consistency I would land on a psalm that aggravated rather than cured my problem....I had missed the main point, which is that the book of Psalms comprises a sampling of spiritual journals much like personal letters to God. I had lacked a lens through which to view the book. I must read them as an "over-the-shoulder" reader since the intended audience was not other people, but God.*[9]

Although I wouldn't want to press it too far, reading and praying all the psalms provides great sessions of what is truly "reality therapy." Somehow we have been able to read the Bible and ignore the difficulties, hardships, and suffering endured by some of the most faithful people in its pages. And they let God know just how unhappy they were with their plight! But they didn't stop there. They came out on the other side of their "faith stretching" experiences with assets they previously didn't have.

Easily ignored are the means by which God's saints have achieved the real blessings of faith. *...we boast in our hope of sharing the glory of God. And not only that, but we also boast in our sufferings, knowing that suffering produces endurance, and endurance produces character, and character produces hope....*(Romans 5:2b-4). What hardly anyone wants to hear and what certainly doesn't make for popular preaching is the hard truth that what God wants for us is the life of faith marked by endurance and character that anchors its hope in the biblical understanding of creation and redemption.

You have to do what has been termed "kangaroo exegesis" (hopping all around in scripture for isolated texts) to arrive at the philosophy of either a prosperity gospel or a formula for achieving a charmed life in a far from charming world. We will deal later in Chapter 8 with some of what it means to be *born from above* (a far better translation I believe than the usual *born again)* but it at least means that God has something far more significant and meaningful for me than what the world usually means by "happiness." To put it plainly: God wants me to be the somebody he has created in his own image, something I can't even begin to approach if my goal in life is the pursuit of happiness, however that is defined but ordinarily with a huge "I" (" happ – I – ness") prominently in the middle of it.

The goal of the true biblical heroes was the pursuit of holiness; but that is the subject for another book since holiness today is usually pictured as a dower, gloomy affair for people who seem to have little life and certainly little joy – and people you definitely don't want to be around. Most of us know certain people we would term "holier than thou" but these bear no resemblance to the biblical meaning of holiness. Taking into account the "totality of the biblical witness" means we pay attention to texts like I Peter 1:13-16:

> *Therefore prepare your minds for action; discipline yourselves; set all your hope on the grace that Jesus Christ will bring you when he is revealed. Like obedient children, do not be conformed to the desires that you formerly had in ignorance. Instead, as he who call you is holy, be holy yourselves in all your conduct; for it is written, "You shall be holy, for I am holy."*

Our Memory System

There are many helpful books on how to use the psalms in your personal prayer life. I will give you a hint of the approach I recommend by giving you a test I recently took – and I got both answers right. In his book *Post-Modern Pilgrims,* Leonard Sweet asks his readers to try an experiment. (This test only "works" for the somewhat older generation.) We are asked to complete two slogans (I have supplied the answers). The first: "Winston tastes good..." ("like a cigarette should.") The second: "Plop, Plop, Fizz, Fizz..." ("oh what a relief it is.") Here is the shocker: the last time these commercials aired was more than thirty-five years ago! Sweet asks us, "How did that message get burned into your brain?"[10]

I know how! They were repeated often enough that they became a part of my memory system. What I need to do is what the psalmists do. In times of uncertainty, questioning, and even doubt, they come back to the great affirmations of faith. In Psalm 22, after expressing a sense of abandonment, we have the affirmations of trust: *...you brought me out of my mother's womb; you made me feel secure on my mother's breast. From birth I was cast on you; from my mother's womb you have been my God.*

An eye for the too often forgotten obvious is that, in praying through the psalms, Psalm 23 follows Psalm 22. We move from *My God, my God, why have you forsaken me?* to *The Lord is my shepherd, I shall not want.* We do so because this is the way life moves. Our goal is to make certain that what becomes a part of our memory system is: *The Lord is my shepherd.*

A simple suggestion: each day take a verse from one of the psalms and use it as your mantra for the day (or week) and repeat it aloud several times during the day. Reading the psalms aloud makes all the difference. For generations people read aloud. Even in school. Even in groups.

If we want to read texts profitably, we should perhaps try to read them as ancient readers did. They read with both eye and ear, and with the lips. That is, they read aloud, or at least half-aloud, even when they read to themselves. This is exactly what the Ethiopian queen's finance minister was doing in Acts 8:26-27, riding along in his chariot somewhere between Jerusalem and Gaza.[11]

It is not possible to choose all the pieces that go into our museum of memories but we can select those things to which we will give preeminence. We can be intentional about those things that will capture our focus, those things that we will continually visit.

Many will recall the legend of Alexander the Great and his famous horse, Bucephalus. No one could ride the horse because it was afraid of its shadow, but Alexander faced it toward the sun – and rode without trouble. The author of a self-help book cites this legend and then gives his advice: "Face toward the sun and the shadows will fall behind you, too."[12]

Not bad advice but we are talking about much more

than positive thinking and positive attitudes. The psalms do not deny the existence of evil and great difficulty. The writers freely express their anxiety, frustration, and even lack of patience with God's seeming inactivity. To these laments there is always an addition. "The spiritual geniuses of the ages and of the everyday don't let despair have the last word. Nor do they close their eyes to its pictures, or deny the enormity of the facts. They say, 'Yes, and....'"[13]

The psalms present life as it really is, the life of faith as it really is, the facts of life as they really are and then they say:

a. Yes, and *I trust in God's unfailing love forever and forever* (52:8).
b. Yes, and *Surely God is my help; the Lord is the one who sustains me* (54:4).
c. Yes, and *in God I trust; I will not be afraid. What can human beings do to me?* (56:11).
d. Yes, and *I will lie down and sleep in peace, for you alone, O Lord, make me dwell in safety* (4:8).
e. Yes, and *Those who know your name will trust in you, for you, Lord, have never forsaken those who seek you* (9:10).
f. Yes, and *The Lord is my light and my salvation – whom shall I fear?* (27:1).

There is no end to the verses you can use to sustain yourself in times of crisis. This is a quantum leap beyond mere positive thinking because these verses come from the hearts and lives of those who had confidence in the God who makes and keeps promises. This is the way Karl Barth defined God: the One who makes and keeps promises.[14] The concept of this kind of a God was absolutely unique in the ancient world. The God revealed in scripture is the God who makes covenants, makes promises and puts his name on the line (his reputation) as the guarantee that he will keep his promises.

I know what the writer of old gospel song meant when he wrote: "Standing on the promises….I'm standing on the promises of God."

A Couple of Exercises

We return to the question from the chapter title, "Who Designed This Prayer Book?" We believe that those who wrote the psalms were inspired by the Spirit of God. So we believe that this prayer book comes to us with divine design. Divine design that provides a timelessness and a timeliness to these ancient prayers and hymns. For the times in which we live, Psalm 46 seems all too appropriate:

> *God is our refuge and strength, an ever-present help in trouble. Therefore we will not fear, though the earth give way and the mountains fall into the heart of the sea. Though its*

But If Not...

waters roar and foam and the mountains quake with their surging (vss. 1-3).

Many spiritual directors have suggested an exercise that comes from verse ten of Psalm 46: *Be still, and know that I am God*....Several times a day, aloud, and very slowly repeat the verse by means of subtraction:

a. *Be still and know that I am God...*
b. Be still and know that I am...
c. Be still and know...
d. Be still...
e. Be...

Another recommended practice is known as *Lectio Divina* – sacred reading.

Paul Jones in *Trumpet at Full Moon* gives a brief summary of this technique. Take a familiar passage of scripture, read it slowly, thoughtfully, aloud. Do it a second time, even slower, savoring the parts. Permit one word or phrase to surface. Keep it. Cherish it. Repeat it as God's word of promise to you during the day.[15]   The first five words of Psalm 23 can be read in this way by emphasizing a different word each time the phrase is repeated:

The Lord is my shepherd.
The *Lord* is my shepherd.
The Lord *is* my shepherd.

The Lord is *my* shepherd.
The Lord is my *shepherd*.

Memorization has almost become a lost art. In every high school literature class, I was required to memorize so much material. Great poetic works, sections from Shakespeare, historical classics like the Gettysburg Address, and famous inspirational writings became an important part of my educational experience. (Of course, there were also selections like "Casey at the Bat" that I will never forget and used only a couple of years ago at a church "Talent Night" to the delight of old and young alike.)

In *Finding Our Way Again: The Return of the Ancient Practices,* Brian McLaren makes these insightful observations:[16]

> *There are times, the ancient way teaches us, when life is so unimaginably hard that stodgy old practices like memorization and recitation can practically save your life, or your sanity.*
>
> *I discovered that learning something by heart can save you when your heart is broken so nothing can come from it except tears, and spontaneity is simply another burden on an already overburdened soul.*
>
> *I read recently about some members of the Christian Peacemaker Teams who were*

kidnapped and held as hostages in Iraq for 188 days. They remarked how the things they memorized had sustained them in their days of terror and boredom.

I know of no other book that has been designed to meet us however and wherever we are. You may not always find yourself in every psalm but you will always find yourself somewhere in the 150. Or should I say, a psalm will find you. This prayer book must have been designed by someone who knows us well and loves us more than we can even begin to fathom.

But If Not...

Reflections

I don't know why we would need a sentence like this to remind us, but we do: "When we realize that the psalmists could address God with absolute honesty, we can take heart and do likewise."[17] When prayer becomes the time of disclosure to God of where we are and how we are, we find no lack of content for our prayers. We find ourselves doing the same kind of praying the psalmists did.

This honesty in praying the psalms also reflects itself in this observation from W. H. Auden: "A real book is not one that we read but one that reads us." The psalmists' calls for vengeance, in often raw and graphic images, challenges me to examine my own dark shadows of resentment, anger, and hostility. Again, in reading the psalms aloud, I find that they read me more often than I would like to admit.

If you don't know where to start in using the psalms, I highly recommend *Answering God: The Psalms as Tools for Prayer* by Eugene Peterson. Published in 1989, it still provides a brief (151 pages), basic, and readable way to read and incorporate the psalms in daily prayer.[18]

If you are worried about repetition and boredom in continuing to use the psalms, I invite you to consider what I have found to be true for me. An ancient adage suggests that there are seventy ways of reading the Bible, one for each year of one's life. We don't remain at the same place so we read with new eyes and a new understanding as the years go by. That makes the Bible forever new and forever a source of new wisdom and insights.

---

[1]Philip Yancey, *The Bible Jesus Read* (Grand Rapids, Zondervan, 1999), 115-116.
[2]David Wolpe, *Why Faith Matters* (New York, HarperOne, 2008), 168.

³Philip Yancey, *The Bible Jesus Read*, 10.
⁴Alden Thompson, *Who's Afraid of the Old Testament God?* (Gonzalez, Florida, Pacesetters, 2003).
⁵Peter Gomes, *The Scandalous Gospel of Jesus* (New York, HarperOne, 2007), 99.
⁶Philip Yancey, *Reaching for the Invisible God* (Grand Rapids, Zondervan, 2000), 73.
⁷Philip Yancey, *The Bible Jesus Read*, 131.
⁸Ibid., 122.
⁹Ibid., 112.
¹⁰Leonard Sweet, *Post-Modern Pilgrims* (Nashville, Broadman & Holman, 2000), 6.
¹¹Jean Paillard, *In Praise of the Inexpressible* (Peabody, Massachusetts, Hendrickson, 2003), 115.
¹²Robert Collier, *The Secret of the Ages* (New York, Jeremy Tarcher Publisher, 2007), 156.
¹³Krista Tippett, *Speaking of Faith* (New York, Viking Books, 2007), 179-180.
¹⁴W. Paul Jones, *A Season in the Desert: Making Time Holy* (Brewster, Paraclete Press, 2000), 107.
¹⁵W. Paul Jones, *Trumpet at Full Moon* (Louisville, John Knox, 1992), 128-129.
¹⁶Brian McLaren, *Finding Our Way Again* (Nashville, Thomas Nelson, 2008), 195, 198.
¹⁷Alden Thompson, *Who's Afraid of the Old Testament God?*, 139.
¹⁸Eugene Peterson, *Answering God* (New York, HarperCollins, 1991).

**Chapter 3:
Who Started the Rumor That Christianity is Easy?**

MODERN OBSERVATIONS:

> *If you have never been frightened by the teachings of Jesus, perhaps you haven't understood them.*[1]

> *The threat of the present new wave of simplistic religion, greater than all the others because the contextual conditions are more favorable to it and the potential consequences more terrible, can be averted only by a widespread attempt within the remnants of formerly "established," "classical" expressions of Christianity to bring doctrine into the streets — not, certainly, as doctrine, but as a struggle to know ourselves in the light of a gospel that penetrates our darkness.*[2]

THE BIBLICAL TEXT: Matthew 10:34-39; John 6:66-68:

> "Do not think that I have come to bring peace to the earth; I have not come to bring peace, but a sword. For I have come to set a man against his father, and a daughter against her mother, and a daughter-in-law against her mother-in-law; and one's foes will be members of one's own household. Whoever loves father or mother more than me is not worthy of me; and whoever loves son or daughter more than me is not worthy of me; and whoever does not take up the cross and follow me is not worthy of me. Those who find their life will lose it, and those who lose their life for my sake will find it."

> Because of this many of his disciples turned back and no longer went about with him. So Jesus asked the twelve, "Do you also wish to go away?" Simon Peter answered him, "Lord, to whom shall we go? You have the words of eternal life."

Jesus on a Bad Day?

I have often wondered if the disciples thought Jesus was just having a bad day. Before he sends them out to proclaim the Gospel, Matthew lets us listen in on his strategy session. The disciples might have felt as I do; it doesn't sound like much of a winning strategy to me! I would have wanted to ask, "Did you get a good night's rest, Jesus? Did one of the Pharisees say something to you yesterday that ticked you off?"

In this strategy session, Jesus talks about bringing a sword, not peace; about setting a person against his family; about taking up a cross; and about losing life in order to find it. They must have wondered what to do. Where is all the stuff about the birds of the air and the flowers of the field and that *"Come unto me all you who labor and are heavy laden and I will give you rest"*? Now that stuff will really sell the Gospel! This other stuff will never play in Galilee!

I can just imagine the scene when a prospective convert asks one of the disciples, "And what does your Rabbi have to offer?" and they rattle off this list of shockers. The response from the prospect most certainly will be, "I think I'll do a little more shopping around." According to our text in John, that is exactly what some of them did: *many of his disciples turned back and no longer went about with him.*

One commentary gives the heading "The Cost of Discipleship" to the text from Matthew 10:34-39 and this comment:

> To the extent that (this passage) seems alien, it is a call to reexamine our own version of Christianity and ask whether we have remade the Christian faith to our own tastes, and whether it is possible to so change faith and have it remain Christian.[3]

Marsha Witten in *All is Forgiven: The Secular Message in American Protestantism,* recounts an afternoon on a Good Friday when the daily mail arrived. She opened the thickest envelope first. It was promotional material for a new church launching in her area. Here is some of that material:[4]

> Hi Neighbor!
>
> At last! A new church for those who have given up on church services! Let's face it. Many people aren't active in church these days. Why?
>
> *****
>
> Too often. . .
>
> --the sermons are boring and don't relate to daily living
> --many churches seem more interested in your wallet than in you

But If Not...

--you wonder about the quality of the nursery care for your little ones.

*****

Do you think attending church should be enjoyable? Well. We've got good news for you!!

*****

Valley Church is a new church designed to meet your needs in the 1990s. At Valley Church you...

--hear positive, practical messages which uplift you each week:

--How to feel good about yourself
--How to overcome depression
--How to have a full and successful life
--Learning to handle your money without it handling you
--The secrets of successful family living
--How to overcome stress.

*****

Trust your children to the care of dedicated nursery workers.

*****

But If Not...

Why not get a lift instead of a letdown this Sunday?

I find the most interesting aspect of all this to be that Marsha Witten describes herself as a non-Christian who does not find this to be good news for her. Is it possible that there is some truly good news after all in Jesus' seemingly puzzling words to his disciples?

A Sword, Not Peace
We begin by looking at the perplexing words *Do not think that I have come to bring peace, but a sword.* Charlie Brown and Pigpen are standing with their elbows on a low wall, looking out over it.

> *Pigpen:* "You never miss the water till the well runs dry. That's what my grandfather always used to say."
>
> *Charlie Brown:* "He must have been a very wise man."
>
> *Pigpen:* "No, that's all he ever said."

Jesus did talk about God's lavish care for the flowers of the field and the birds of the air and how much he cares for us. Jesus did say that those who are themselves heavy laden could find rest in him. BUT THAT IS NOT ALL HE SAID. Jesus was not a Johnnie-one-note in his proclamation. His faith was a symphony.
It is possible to lift out of the Gospels and the Bible as

a whole passages that can be printed on small cards and put into a "Comfort Box." (I was once given such a box as a gift.) I suppose there is nothing wrong with that – except it better not be the only box in your faith. One minister writes: "Forgive us preachers for presenting the Christian life as a matter of faith development, slow, orderly growth toward the goal of psychic wellness. Painless therapy, not major surgery. Things are messier than that, more costly. We were buried with him in baptism."[5]

Too many people never expect to hear anything on the lips of Jesus except the word *Shalom* (peace); they are shocked when they hear a word like *sword*. I have an acid test for a biblical sermon: a biblical sermon is one that is true to the text in the context of the entire Bible. That is why genuine biblical preaching is such a tough job. When I preach anything Jesus said, I must speak to it in the context of everything he said. I must always be aware of the question that won't go away: "Yes, that is true. But what else is also true?"

Luke 12:51 records the same event and teaching that Matthew gives and uses another word in place of *sword*: *"Do you think that I have come to bring peace to the earth? No, I tell you, but rather division."* Either translation means that the moment you decide to become a disciple of Jesus Christ you will find yourself in conflict with many of the ways of the world and with many aspects of the culture in which you live.

Jesus, in speaking of priorities, loyalties, and commitments, warns that a person's faith cannot take a back seat even to family. I will quickly add that I really do believe we become better children, spouses, parents, and family members when we have a basic faith-commitment at the center of our lives. I believe this enables us to be focused and enables us to make other commitments.

I think the disciples did have some understanding of what Jesus meant when he said, "If it comes down to faith or family, it has to be faith." For the vast majority of us, it has not meant that; it did mean that for many, especially those in the Roman world who were the first recipients of the written Gospels.

In our reflection on these passages of scripture, I believe the emphasis should be on the two questions, the first asked by Jesus and the second asked by Peter: *"Do you also wish to go away?" "Lord, to whom shall we go? You have the words of eternal life."*

The real question is not: What will something cost? but, Is it worth it? The real question is not: How inconvenient will this be? but, How much do I really want and need this? The question is not: How can I coast through life and be most comfortable while avoiding most challenges and risks? but, How can I get the most out of life, use my gifts and talents, and become who I believe God intends me to become? That is just the tip of the iceberg when attempting to discover the real questions real life offers us. The problem with the current prosperity gospel is that it has little to do with the true riches of the Kingdom of God that Jesus talked about. The basic problem underlying so much of the easy-faith propaganda and user-friendly church stuff that I read and hear about is that it borders on what one writer has called "Christless Christianity."

When you read the Gospels, you discover that Jesus gave one basic invitation: "Follow me." Which means: "Become my disciple." Unfortunately, what we have heard so often is true: "We have been much better at making converts than we have been at making disciples." Perhaps one of the places we have gotten off-track is in a misreading of Matthew 28:19-20. It is commonly called The Great Commission and reads like this in the familiar *King James* translation:

> *Go ye therefore, and teach all nations, baptizing them in the name of the Father, and of the Son, and of the Holy Ghost: Teaching them to observe all things whatsoever I have commanded you: and, lo, I am with you always, even unto the end of the world. Amen*

In the original Greek, there are three participles and one verb in this command from our Lord. The participles are: *going, teaching, and baptizing.* The one verb can be translated *make disciples.* So the text reads: *Going (as you go), make disciples, baptizing and teaching obedience to all the commands I have given you* (adapted from *The New Living Translation*).

Sidebar: I call these closing verses from Matthew "The Great Promise." Matthew begins his gospel with the prophecy from Isaiah confirming that the son to be born to Mary will be called Immanuel which he tells us means *God is with us.* He closes his gospel with Jesus' final words to his followers: *And be sure of this: I am with you always, even to the end of the age* (New Living Translation).

Discipleship means we take seriously what Jesus has called all of his followers to be and to do. Jesus' Sermon on

But If Not...

the Mount is a description of the way Kingdom of God people live, the way his disciples live. Someone has given this brief summary of Matthew 5 through 7:[6]

    a.   Be light (5:14-16).
    b.   Seek reconciliation (5:23-24).
    c.   Keep the commitments you make (5:27-30).
    d.   Mean what you say and say what you mean (5:37)
    e.   Don't retaliate (5:38-42).
    f.   Love your enemies (5:43-45).
    g.   Don't show off your faith (6:1).
    h.   Know what's important and what's not (6:19-21).
    i.   Put God first (6:33).
    j.   Measure yourself the way you measure others (7:1-2).
    k.   Treat others the way you want to be treated (7:12).

None of this sounds very easy to me! I thought I would never find the perfect prayer that spoke exactly to where I am and exactly to what I need. The author who gives it says it's his favorite prayer of petition and he has lost the source of it. Whatever the source, it is now my favorite daily prayer of petition:[7]

> *Dear God, so far today I've done all right. I haven't gossiped. I haven't lost my temper. I haven't been greedy or grumpy or nasty or selfish. In fact, I haven't done anything*

wrong at all. I'm really pleased about all that. But, God, in a just a few minutes I'll be getting out of bed, and from then on, I'll be needing lots of help. Amen.

Staying in Tune With Reality

If Christianity is so tough and involves such a struggle, why be a disciple? Lloyd Douglas, author of several novels including *The Robe*, lived in a boarding house when he was a university student. On the first floor resided a retired music teacher, infirm and unable to leave his apartment. Every morning they had a ritual: Douglas would come down the steps, open the old man's door and ask, "Well, what's the good news?" The other would pick up his tuning fork, tap it on the side of his wheelchair, and say, "That's middle C! It was middle C yesterday; it will be middle C tomorrow; it will be middle C a thousand years from now. The tenor upstairs sings flat, the piano across the hall is out of tune, but, my friend, that is middle C! The old man had discovered a constant reality on which he could depend, an unchanging truth to which he could cling.

The writer who gives that story, then adds this comment: "Jesus Christ is our tuning fork, ringing out middle C in a cacophonous world of competing truths; his pitch defines tonal reality and sets every other note in it proper place."[8]

Christianity is not easy, but where else can I go to be in tune with reality? Where else can I go to know that I am in harmony with the purposes of the universe, the dimensions of eternity?

Is Christianity easy? No. Is it worth it? Absolutely, no doubt about it!

But If Not...

Reflections

Douglas John Hall's trilogy, *Christian Theology in a North American Context: Thinking the Faith; Professing the Faith; and Confessing the Faith*, is neither a quick or easy read but it is extremely worthwhile for those willing to invest some time in pursuing a quality and basic theological education. His favorite term for church is "The Disciple Community."[9] A return to this biblical description is the best identity statement for today's church that I have found.

I preached a sermon once titled "Are the Beatitudes the Happitudes?" In his setting for the sermon, Matthew tells us that *When Jesus saw the crowds, he went up the mountain; and after he sat down, his disciples came to him.* When a Rabbi sat to teach, everyone knew immediately it was official teaching. Jesus sent a clear signal that what he was about to teach was crucial, central, important – not to be missed. He begins the sermon by describing the kind of person he calls truly blessed. The problem with translating the first word in the Beatitudes as *happy* is that the translation is not rich or deep enough. *Blessed* carries with it the favor and affirmation of God; these blessings are gifts, not achievements. It designates those who are in line with the purposes and ways of God's will in heaven and on earth (as in the prayer Jesus' gave his disciples as the Model Prayer, what we call The Lord's Prayer: *Thy kingdom come, thy will be done on earth as it is in heaven*).

Taking Jesus seriously can easily lead one into high risk territory. I give this account without comment:[10]

The rector of a large Episcopal parish recently told me the story of what happened when, in obedience to Jesus' teaching that we should pray for our enemies, he put Saddam Hussein on the prayer list at a Sunday service at the onset of the Gulf War. Three people stormed out of the church, the senior warden was apoplectic, and the congregation was in an uproar. The rector said it was the most genuinely frightening time of his life. The only thing that saved us, he said, was the brevity of the Gulf War.

---

[1] Thomas Bruno, *Jesus, Ph.D. Psychologist* (Alachua, Florida, Bridge-Logos Publishers, 2000), 295.
[2] Douglas Hall, *Thinking the Faith* (Minneapolis, Augsburg, 1989), 235.
[3] *The New Interpreter's Bible* (Nashville, Abingdon Press, 1996), VII, 261, 263.
[4] Marsha Witten, *All Is Forgiven: The Secular Message in American Protestantism* (Princeton, Princeton University Press, 1995).
[5] William Willimon, *Peculiar Speech* (Grand Rapids, Eerdmans Publishing, 1992), 15-16.
[6] Jan G. Linn, *Big Christianity* (Louisville, Westminster John Knox, 2006), 16-17.
[7] Leonard Sweet, *The Three Hardest Words in the World to Get Right* (Colorado Springs, Waterbrook Press, 2006), 71.
[8] Donald McCullough, *The Trivialization of God* (Colorado Springs, Navpress, 1995), 66-67.
[9] Douglas Hall, *Thinking the Faith,* 128.

[10] Fleming Rutledge, *Not Ashamed of the Gospel* (Grand Rapids, Eerdmans Publishing, 2007), 102.

But If Not...

Part I: Reality 101
Points to Ponder

To feel that God is not living up to his good reputation is one of the most poignant, inescapable experiences the saints ever face.

Be bold and mighty forces will come to your aid.

Many who name it and claim it never get it.

The psalms teach us to pray our inner conflicts and contradictions.

Faith stretching experiences appear to be the common experience for most of us.

Reading and praying all of the psalms provide great lessons in reality therapy.

Reading the psalms aloud makes all the difference.

God is the one who makes and keeps promises.

A real book is not one that we read but one that reads us.

Is Jesus simply having a bad day when he gives his strategy session in Matthew 10?

Whenever we affirm any truth, we always need to ask, "What else is also true?"

Does the fact that The Great Commission (Matthew 28:19-20) contains only one verb tell us anything about priorities?

The blessings promised in the Beatitudes are gifts, not achievements.

Part II:
RESPONSIBILITY, NOT RESULTS
Chapter 4: You Are Among the Called

MODERN OBSERVATIONS:

The church exists so that God has a place to point people toward a purpose as big as their capabilities, and to help them identify all the ways they flee from that high call.[1]

By moving against our calls, we move against ourselves.[2]

William Barclay: "There are two important moments in your life: the moment you are born and the moment you discover why."

At the end of the day, God will not ask you why you didn't lead someone else's life or invest someone else's gifts. He will not ask, "What did you do with what you didn't have?" Though, he will ask, "What did you do with what you had?"[3]

THE BIBLICAL TEXT: Ephesians 4:1-6:

> *I therefore, the prisoner of the Lord, beg you to lead a life worthy of the calling to which you have been called, with all humility and gentleness, with patience, bearing with one another in love, making every effort to maintain the unity of the Spirit in the bond of peace. There is one body and one Spirit, just as you were called to the one hope of your calling, one Lord, one faith, one baptism, one God and Father of all, who is above all and through all and in all.*

The Great "Therefore"

I had never really thought about it, but I like the suggestion I once read: "The cute little yellow buttons with the smiling face and the legend 'Smile, God loves you' might be more accurate if the mouth and eyes reflected a bit more apprehension, and the message said, 'Watch out! God loves you.'"[4] For me, this denotes response – ability.

This is exactly what Paul is calling for when he uses a very simple word, one of the most important words he ever uses. In Ephesians 4 we find the same great transitional word he uses in Romans 12: *I THEREFORE the prisoner in the Lord; I appeal to you, THEREFORE, brothers and sisters...*THEREFORE is the challenge of response – ability.

Preceding this word in Ephesians you have the chapters dealing with what has been called "God's drama of salvation."[5] This great drama of salvation has to do with the gift of God's son, crucified and resurrected for our salvation, and summarized in the phrase *by grace you have been saved* (Ephesians 2:5). Or, to paraphrase, "Watch out! God loves you!"

Following the word *therefore* in both Romans and Ephesians we have what is known as the ethical material: instructions on how people are to live. The order of things is clear: first a recognition and reception of the wonderful things God has done to bring human beings into a right relationship with himself, then, and only then, instructions on how to live in the light of this newly found grace.

But, alas, even Paul with his great *therefore* found it necessary to use phrases like *I beg you, I beseech you, I implore you*....

Everyone Has a Gift, Everyone Has a Calling

In a *Frank and Earnest* cartoon, Frank is standing in front of a booth talking to a man over whose head is the sign "Career Counselor." Frank is saying, "I couldn't decide whether I wanted to be on the fast track or the slow track, so I've just been hanging around the station."

Even in Paul's day there were a lot of Christians who were not on track, they were just hanging around the station. In our day, I think those of us in ministry must bear a lot of the responsibility for the hanging around the station. We have not been as effective as we should have been in our proclamation of the Gospel for the converted. One author makes what I see as a necessary distinction:

> *In an exploration of the inner sphere of the person, one has to begin somewhere, and I have chosen to begin where Christ appears to have begun – with the distinction between the called and the driven....Are we driven people, propelled by the winds of our times, pressed to conform or compete? Or are we called people, the recipients of the gracious beckoning of Christ when he promises to make us into something?[6]*

Some boys and girls were asked what they thought Adam and Even did in the Garden of Eden. Here are some of their answers:[7]

    a. Krista, age 8: "They played tag. It was simple enough to learn. Even a snake could play."
    b. Craig, age 12: "Probably they took long walks in the new moonlight that God had created and tried to figure out what to do about loneliness. That's when they decided to have the first children."
    c. Peggy, age 10: "Adam and Eve played bingo and the churches picked up on it later on."
    d. Jerome, age 9: "They had deep talks about what they were there for….People have been trying to figure that out ever since."

I believe the place to begin in trying to figure out what we are here for is with the biblical premise that everyone has a calling and everyone has a gift. Paul's words in Ephesians are written, not to clergy, but as 1:1 tells us: *to all the saints in Ephesus.* Here is another good word to reclaim for our faith; Paul always addresses believers (those in the church) as saints. Here is what he writes to ALL the saints in Ephesus and to all of us: (*Revised English Bible* translation):

   a. *I implore you...as God has called you, live up to your calling (4:1).*
   b. *...each of us has been given a special gift, a particular share in the bounty of Christ (4:7).*

When someone asks him, "When did you receive your calling?" a minister writes that he always responds: "I'm still receiving it." And then he makes these insightful observations:[8]

> *The call by the lake that Simon and Andrew received from Jesus was a call to discipleship and a call to be "fishers of men and women." All of us receive the same call today, no matter how we choose to live it. Truck drivers and mail-persons alike. Like Simon and Andrew, I got my call by the water, too. The nets I left to pursue that call were the ones that had entangled my life in destructive and selfish ways.*
> *Leaving them behind freed me to follow in a way not possible while tethered in their web. But "Come follow me" weren't words I heard once, and then the path was set. I kept hearing them. And now there are other nets*

But If Not...
from which I must cut myself loose.

The call and gifts for ministry Paul gives in his listing in Ephesians 4:11-12 is not meant to be the exclusive list of those who are called and those who are gifted. Paul asserts that every Christian is called and every Christian is gifted. One commentator writes what I have always believed: "There are no exceptions, for all in the church are members of (Christ's) body and as such endowed with some gift-by-grace (charisma)."[9]

Unfortunately, here is a necessary sidebar: In our day when many are opting out of church membership and feel that nothing is lost in making that decision, it may be time to do a little basic church theology. The New Testament never speaks of church membership, it speaks about being "members of the body." In a book with the subtitle "Mapping the DNA of Christ's Body," the author puts it succinctly: "We speak today of membership rather than bodyship, which shows that most North American Christians are simply blind to the differences between the biblical and contemporary meanings of "member."[10]

As Paul contends (a preacher is reported to have added, "and rightly so!"), all members of the body of Christ have a unique calling and are challenged to live up to that calling. The entire concept of "calling" for too long has been applied only to those in "religious" vocations. Asked what he did for a living, one man routinely replied, "I'm an ordained plumber." This brings to mind the Garrison Keillor quote: "Writing is a sacred calling – but so are gardening, dentistry, and plumbing – so don't put on airs."

To get up every day and know you are doing what God has called you to do makes all the difference in your life and in your world. There ought to be a sense of call in whatever one attempts to do in life. (We'll deal more with this concept in Chapter 11.) One of the basic problems with the idea of calling is that it is often associated with the dramatic and spectacular – like Moses at the burning bush or Paul on the Damascus road. For most of us this is never going to happen. That doesn't mean we don't have a calling. In an excellent book simply titled *Callings* the author gives these encouraging words: "Most of the calls we receive and ignore are the proverbial still, small voices...the daily calls to pay attention to our intuitions, to be authentic....We ought not to spend so much time awaiting booming voices from on high that we stumble over the whispers that are right at our feet."[11]

The Challenge

I have seen this challenge ascribed to various sources, including mountain wisdom, but whatever the point of origination, it states the obvious in way that cannot be missed: "Be what you is, not what you ain't, cause if you ain't what you is, you is what you ain't."

Andrew Greeley is a Catholic priest and author who

But If Not...

writes what some consider unusual stories for one in his vocation. In his *Confessions,* he packs more healthy psychology and theology into three paragraphs than I have found anywhere else. This is one of those pieces for meditation, reflection, and group discussion:[12]

> *Fortunately for me, my parents' emphasis on effort rather than outcome – and powerful praise for effort – dispensed me permanently from the obligation to be perfect. So I was freed by my parents, to a considerable extent anyway, of the need of perfectionism and of envious resentment of those who were better than I was – wonderful blessings because they have made it easy to distinguish between myself and my work.*
>
> *I am not James Joyce (or) Agatha Christie....In fact, one could fill the pages of a book with a list of authors and artists that I am not. But so what? Why need I be any of those people? And more to the point, why should my work be evaluated against theirs? I write the kind of stories I can write and that I like to write, stories which I design to be comedies of grace....Why is it necessary to be Graham Greene or James Joyce? Why isn't it enough*

to be me?

Some readers may think that it is an absurd position to take. The point here is that I was raised to think that way. My parents were content with me if I tried to do as well as I could what I was able to do. I wasn't compared with others whether they were more gifted than I or less gifted….That seems like sound common sense, sound psychology and sound Christianity.

In his admonition to live a life worthy of the calling to which we have been called, Paul adds some very important words: *…with all humility and gentleness, with patience, bearing with one another in love, making every effort to maintain the unity of the Spirit in the bond of peace.* Another way to translate that first phrase is: *making allowances for one another because you love one another* (J. B. Phillips translation).

It has always taken real courage to be authentically yourself and live authentically the calling you feel you have received. We ought to provide the space, encouragement, and freedom for each individual to respond to the way each believes God is working in his or her life. We generally spend more time being critical of one another that we do being encouraging of one another in our God given uniqueness. I think that may indeed be one of the reasons so many believers spend so much time just hanging around the station. If you don't ever get on a train people can't say you're on the wrong one!

My encouragement is: Take the risk! Get on track! Even if you get on the wrong train, you can get off at the next station, and get on another one!

On a Yorkshire tombstone are these words: "God give me work – Till my life shall end – and life – Till my work is done." According to what we believe to be words of Holy Scripture, that is exactly what God will do...because *You Are Among the Called!*

But If Not...

Reflections

In writing this chapter there was a real temptation to overdo the amount of quoted material (which I may have done). One reason for that temptation is because I know of so many who have said so many things so much better than I can say them. One safeguard was that there wasn't enough space to explore too many of the ramifications of the concept of calling.

There is a final observation I want to give from the pen of Walter Brueggemann. He cites Jesus' invitation in Matthew 11:28 (*Come to me, all you that are weary and are carrying heavy burdens, and I will give you rest*) with this commentary:[13]

> *But what is it that makes people like us weary? It is not working too hard that makes us weary. It is rather, I submit, living a life that is against the grain of our true creatureliness, living a ministry that is against the grain of our true vocation, being placed in a false position so that our day-to-day operation requires us to contradict what we know best about ourselves and what we love most about our life as children of God. Exhaustion comes from the demand that we be, in some measure, other than we truly are; such alienation requires too much energy to navigate.*

To which I will simply add: Amen and Amen!

[1] Barbara Brown Taylor, *Speaking of Sin* (Cambridge, Cowley Publications, 2000), 85.
[2] Gregg Levoy, *Callings* (New York, Three Rivers Press, 1997), 34.
[3] John Ortberg, *If You Want To Walk On Water, You've Got To Get Out Of The Boat* (Grand Rapids, Zondervan, 2001), 43.
[4] William Frey, *The Dance of Hope* (Colorado Springs, Waterbrook Press, 2003), 34.
[5] *The Interpreter's Bible* (Nashville, Abingdon Press, 1952), X, 682.
[6] Gordon MacDonald, *Restoring Joy* (Nashville, Thomas Nelson, 2005), 9, 29.
[7] Thomas Heller, *Just Build the Ark and the Animals Will Come* (New York, Villard Books, 1994), 15.
[8] Edward Beck, *God Underneath* (New York, Image Books, 2002), 58-59.
[9] *The Broadman Bible Commentary* (Nashville, Broadman Press, 1969), XI, 155.
[10] Howard Snyder, *Decoding the Church* (Grand Rapids, Baker Books, 2002), 52.
[11] Gregg Levoy, *Callings,* 5, 23.
[12] Andrew Greeley, *Confessions of a Parish Priest* (New York, Simon and Schuster, 1986), 46-47.
[13] Walter Brueggemann, *Mandate to Difference* (Louisville, Westminster John Knox, 2007), 42.

Chapter 5: Who Am I That I Should Do It?

MODERN OBSERVATIONS:

Whether you think you can or you can't, you're probably right.

- Henry Ford

Yes, I decided to be a preacher, and the decision preceded final proof. The truth is, there is no final proof. One can toss the fleece, as did Gideon (Judges 6:36-40), not once, not twice, not a thousand times, and have the undeniable proof. Sooner or later one has to decide, unless, of course, one wishes to make a career of fleece tossing. But then that, too, is a decision.[1]

I've been studying Joseph Campbell's books on the hero's journey in myth and story. He says that the only way to be a hero is to prepare and be ready when the moment comes. You can't pick ahead of time which dragon you'll slay.²

God called Moses: "Go to Pharaoh – the most powerful man on earth. Tell him to let his labor forces leave without compensation to worship a God he doesn't believe in. Then convince a stiff-necked people to run away into the desert. That's your calling." And Moses said, "Here am I. Send Aaron."³

THE BIBLICAL TEXT: Exodus 3:9-12:

> "The cry of the Israelites has now come to me; I have also seen how the Egyptians oppress them. So come, I will send you to Pharaoh to bring my people, the Israelites, out of Egypt." But Moses said to God, "Who am I that I should go to Pharaoh, and bring the Israelites out of Egypt?" He said, "I will be with you; and this shall be sign that it is I who sent you: when you have brought the people out of Egypt, you shall worship God on this mountain."

Missed Humor

The situation is so serious that it is easy to miss the humor in this dialogue between Moses and God.

When Joseph brings his father and brothers down into Egypt, it is to save them from starvation. Not only are they well fed, but with Joseph in a position of power second only to Pharaoh, they enjoy a privileged status and they prosper in every way. All goes exceedingly well for many years until we are told that *a new king arose over Egypt who did not know Joseph* (Exodus 1:8). The Hebrews have so multiplied that they are viewed as a threat to the Egyptian nation. The solution to the problem is to demote them to the position of slaves.

And slavery of the worst kind is described in the opening verses of Exodus: *The Egyptians became ruthless in imposing tasks on the Israelites and made their lives bitter with hard service in mortar and brick and in every kind of field labor. They were ruthless in all the tasks that they imposed on them* (1:13-14). So God's people do what God's people have always done. They pray and cry out daily to God for deliverance. Finally, after many generations, God responds. From a burning bush God calls, "Moses, Moses." In his first direct speech in the book of Exodus, God tells Moses, "*I have seen...I have heard...I have known...I have come down*" (3:7-8).

Moses' initial response must have been, "Hallelujah! At last!" He couldn't contain his excitement until God says, "So I'm sending YOU to Pharaoh to bring my people out of

Egypt." And Moses' says, "What?!" (Not in the text, but I see strong implications for its inclusion!) Surely God has misunderstood the situation; doesn't he realize how ridiculous his suggestion is? Moses with a shepherd's staff against the horses and chariots of the armies of Egypt is strictly no contest. Moses thought GOD was going to do something! That is why Moses responds as we all would have responded: *Who am I that I should go to Pharaoh, and bring the Israelites out of Egypt?*

Moses would have given a hearty "Amen" to this limerick I have seen posted at various places:

> *They told him the job couldn't be done.*
> *He rolled up his sleeves and went to it.*
> *He tackled the job that couldn't be done.*
> *...and he couldn't do it.*

In our world as in Moses' world, there seems to be much wrong that we are certain can only be righted by divine intervention. We moan, cry out, carry on, wring our hands, certain that the end of all things is at hand. Suddenly we hear God saying, *"I have seen...I have heard...I have known...I have come down. I'm going to do something about this mess. I am sending YOU to DO it."* We immediately find ourselves echoing the words of Moses, "Who am I, that I should do it?" The biblical story has become our story.

The Called Versus The Un-called Life

As in Chapter 4, we are talking about the difference

between the called and the un-called life. This distinction makes all the difference in the world. I can't think of any time in our history when we are more in need of this reminder:

> *This extended narrative (in Exodus) invites reflection upon the nature of vocation, and the power of "call" in the life of faith. An uncalled life is an autonomous existence in which there is no intrusion, disruption, or redefinition, no appearance or utterance of the Holy. We may imagine in our autonomous existence, moreover, that no one knows our name until we announce it, and no one requires anything of us except that for which we volunteer. The life of Moses in this narrative, as the lives of all people who live in this narrative of faith, is not autonomous. There is this One who knows and calls by name, even while we imagine we are unknown and unsummoned.*[4]

A more earthy description of the problem is found in this dialogue between Linus and Charlie Brown:

> *Linus: " I don't like to face problems head on. I think the best way to solve problems is to avoid them. This is a distinct philosophy of*

mine. No problem is so big or so complicated that it can't be run away from."

Charlie Brown: "What if everyone was like you? What if we all ran away from our problems? Huh? What then? What if everyone in the whole world suddenly decided to run away from his problems?"

Linus: "Well, at least we'd all be running in the same direction!"

God says to Moses who had run away from Egypt, "You are to go and face the problem and do something about it. I have called you to do it." Through this calling, God was not only going to save his people, God was going to save Moses. It is this sense of call, this sense of vocation, that saves all of us. Somewhere I found and saved this paragraph from Mike Yaconelli:

> Jesus died on the cross to save us from sin, sure. But I would suggest that he also saved us from meaningless, boring, predictable, shallow, empty, dehumanizing work. I am convinced that what characterizes people who know Jesus is not their lack of sin, but the presence of a radical, wild, mysterious calling from God.

I have always found it helpful to keep several books going at once. Along with daily scripture reading, I try to read something that is considered a "weighty tome," something that deals with the practice of ministry, a theological work, and something that can be classified as "inspirational." (Note: I usually end the day with a good mystery. As of this writing I am reading one of the great classics in this field, *Trent's Last Case* by E. C. Bentley.) One of my favorite inspirational reads of several years ago remains on my book shelf: Arthur Gordon's *A Touch of Wonder*. In this book, Gordon tells of meeting an old man on the marshes of the Georgia Coast. Here are some excerpts from that encounter:

> *He nodded at the two or three fish in my boat and asked, "Think you could teach me how to catch those?" Ordinarily, I was wary of strangers, but anyone interested in fishing was hardly a stranger....I gave him a hand line and showed him how to bait his hooks with fiddler crabs....I was tempted to ask where he was from; there was a crispness in the way he spoke that was different from the soft accents I was accustomed to. But I didn't. He had said he was a teacher, though, and so I asked him what he taught.*
>
> *"In the school catalogue they call it English," he said. "But I like to think of it as a course in magic – in the mystery and magic of words....Words, just little black marks on*

paper. Just sounds in empty air. But think of the power they have! They can make you laugh or cry, love or hate, fight or run away. They can heal or hurt." [5]

Those of us who have been fortunate enough to have teachers like this have been greatly blessed. It is obvious this man had found his calling, his place, his niche to fill, the thing for which he was born. He had turned what some have made a labor with little love into something that was filled with a touch of wonder. (More about our "small" callings in the next chapter.)

I Am Not Moses

The unvoiced question that is always on the horizon when this text from Exodus is read is: "I can understand how the called life was for Moses, but I'm no Moses." My initial response is always: Moses didn't know he was Moses until God got through with him! Does it sound too much like "preaching" when I say that none of us knows who we are until God gets through with us? Most people I know are much too modest about the possibilities for accomplishment in their lives. I have never thought it was helpful to tell a child, "You can be anything you want to be." I immediately want to shout, "No, you can't! But you can be what God has gifted you to be, what God is calling you to be, what is suited to where you are and who you are and what is needed to be done by you in your world."

But If Not...

What Moses does is to respond to the calling that comes to him. All we are supposed to do is to respond to the calling that comes to us. Henry Van Dyke gave advice that still stands: "Use what talents you possess: the woods would be very silent if no birds sang except those that sang best." Many get discouraged and despair about their callings because they are continually comparing themselves with others.

Another of my highly recommend reads is Brennan Manning's *The Ragamuffin Gospel*. (If someone doesn't feel encouraged and motivated by this book, my unspoken thought is: "You're a wet match that can't be sparked!" I read that line somewhere and cannot get it out of my memory bank because it is helpful when dealing with unresponsive persons – especially after you have given it a 200% effort.) Here is a single sentence that is worth memorizing:

> *We should be astonished at the goodness of God, stunned that He should bother to call us by name, our mouths wide open at His love, bewildered that at this very moment we are standing on holy ground.*[6]

Underlying Moses' question "Who am I that I should do it?" is the deeper question, "How can I do it? By whose authority and with whose equipping power can I do it?"

But If Not...

Moses was right to be reluctant. Years before, he had tried his hand at deliverance. His flight from Egypt resulted from his killing an Egyptian taskmaster who was beating a Hebrew slave. To return to Egypt was a high risk venture. After all, it was Moses and not God who would be standing face to face with Pharaoh. The text used as the basis for this chapter contains a Hebrew sentence that can be translated in two ways:

> a. *This shall be the sign for you that it is I who sent you: when you have brought the people out of Egypt, you shall worship God on this mountain. The sign comes after the event. The sign will be a successful exodus from Egypt.*
> b. *Or you can read the sentence: I will be with you and this shall be the sign for you. The sign is the presence of God. Here is the authority and the power to accomplish what God is asking. Here is the reason it can be done.*

I immediately think of Paul's *I can do all things through Christ who strengthens me* (Philippians 4:13). I don't believe Paul is boasting that he is able to do anything he decides to do. I believe he is saying, "I have the power to do what I am called to do." When Moses asks, "Who am I?"

God's answer is: "You may not feel like much, but, Moses, in relation to me you are somebody. You are really somebody: you are deliverer, prophet, law giver."

Having an eye (and ear) for the obvious, I spell it out. When we ask God, "Who am I?" God gives us the same answer. "You may not feel like much, but in relation to me you are somebody. You are really somebody. You are...." And that is where he issues our call, our vocation, our reason for being. My rule of thumb for callings: the called can always count on the presence of the caller. Our sun is just one star in the Milky Way Galaxy, a spiral of a trillion stars. It is estimated that there are fifty billion galaxies in the universe. The One who says, "I will be with you," is the God of the galaxies.

Many churches observe the annual "All Saints Day." There are many definitions for what exactly it is that makes one a special saint to be revered by the church at large. I like this definition best: "All saints become saints by fulfilling those duties themselves to which they have been called."[7] This degree of sainthood is possible for all of us, all that is required is that we fulfill those duties to which we have been called. What is best of all is that you won't have to ask, "Who am I?" As you live out your calling you will know you are one of God's saints.

But If Not...

Reflections

To maintain a proper self-perspective, the Talmud teaches that every human being should wear a jacket with two pockets. In one, the rabbis say, should be a stone inscribed, "I am but dust and ashes." In the other pocket should be a stone inscribed, "For my sake the world was made." Each stone should be used as we need it.[8]

My experience has been that most people I know aren't struggling with pride and arrogance but are lost in the question, "Who am I that I CAN do it?" I continue to believe that whatever God calls us to do he will equip us to do, he will enable us to do. This certainly does not mean without hard work, effort, setbacks, disappointments, detours – you name it. I'm not ruling out the difficulties involved in any endeavor. Moses' experience in the exodus was no stroll through the park – it was a forty year wilderness experience – with the incessant murmuring from the very people he had rescued from slavery. (I have often thought that, if I had been in Moses' place, I would have done a whole lot more than hit that rock with a stick. I fear that my striking would not have been restricted to an inanimate object! If you have forgotten the story, read Numbers 20:1-13.)

Samuel Rutherford's "Duty is ours; events are God's" is another reminder of where we are in the scheme of things and the clarion call to always be aware of the need to do what we can do and then let it go. Outcomes belong in

God's hands. Once I can grant God his territory of "results," and keep myself busy in my territory of daily deeds, I am freed from the demon of "success." Mother Teresa's philosophy of the call to faithfulness and not success kept her ministry going against all the odds in Calcutta. All the parables Jesus ever told about the final judgment come down to being faithful. None are about being successful.

If you are having trouble discovering exactly what you ought to be about, I have no easy answer but I do have an approach that I follow. (More specifics will come in Part V.) "As human beings, our tendency is to tell life to listen for what we want....Your life will work much better once you begin to listen to life."[9] To be "on the listen" is to keep an open stance as we live. When we do, I believe God's Spirit always finds a way to get through to us. There is always the feeling of great joy and satisfaction when we can say, "Yes, I should do that...and with God's help, I can do that."

---

[1] Fred Craddock, *Reflections on My Call to Preach* (St. Louis, Chalice Press, 2009), 116-117.

[2] Richard Rohr, *Near Occasions of Grace* (Maryknoll, New York, Orbis Books, 1993), 112.

[3] John Ortberg, *If You Want To Walk On Water, You've Got To Get Out Of The Boat*, 69.

[4] *The New Interpreter's Bible*, I, 719.

[5] Arthur Gordon, *A Touch of Wonder* (Carmel, Guideposts Associates, 1974), 58-59.

⁶Brennan Manning, *The Ragamuffin Gospel* (Sisters, Oregon, Multnomah Publishers, 2000), 102.

⁷Jean-Pierre De Caussade, *The Sacrament of the Present Moment* (San Francisco, Harper & Row, 1982), 57.

⁸Philip Yancey, *Reaching for the Invisible God,* 90.

⁹Robin Sharma, *Discover Your Destiny With the Monk Who Sold His Ferrari* (New York, HarperOne, 2006), 37.

Chapter 6: Doing Some Simple Thing

MODERN OBSERVATIONS:

> *William Sloan Coffin once preached a sermon on David and Goliath. He caught the attention of the congregation when he put these words into the mouth of the great giant, clad in all his armor and towering over the little boy: "Hey, kid, whatcha got in the bag?"[1]*

> *How did the Salvation Army get so much favorable publicity out of the First World War? They were a comparatively small part of the "Services" that catered to the boys "over there" and yet they carried off the lion's share of the glory. Do you know how they did it?   By concentrating on one thing – DOUGHNUTS! They served doughnuts to the boys – and they did it well.[2]*

> *Our lives are measured out in coffee spoons, wrote T. S. Eliot; they are measured out not in grand sweeps but in small gestures.[3]*

THE BIBLICAL TEXT: II Kings 5:10-14:

> *Elisha sent a messenger to him, saying, "Go, wash in the Jordan seven times, and your flesh shall be restored and you shall be clean." But Naaman became angry and went away, saying, "I thought that for me he would surely come out, and stand and call on the name of the Lord his God, and would wave his hand over the spot, and cure the leprosy! Are not Abana and Pharpar, the rivers of Damascus, better than all the waters of Israel? Could I not wash in them, and be clean?" He turned and went away in a rage. But his servants approached and said to him, "Father, if the prophet had commanded you to do something difficult, would you not have done it? How much more, when all he said to you was, 'Wash and be clean'?" So he went down and immersed himself seven times in the Jordan, according to the word of the man of God; his flesh was restored like the flesh of a young boy, and he was clean.*

Not Trying Too Hard

It has been reported that there are over 20,000 distinct web sites that address the subject of information overload![4] The writer who gives this information, then gives instructions on how to install and use filters. He even suggests that we engage in what he calls "creative ignorance and inattention." His challenge is, for a part of every day, live inside an "information-free zone" by turning off televisions, cell phones, beepers, radios, and e-mail/web-based communication. His basic line is: "Keep your information technology at a manageable minimum."[5]

All this is contained in a book titled *NOT TRYING TOO HARD*. Although this is a book designed for pastors and congregations, its wisdom is applicable to every individual. Its basic lesson I learned the hard way over the long haul: in trying to be everything to everybody we often wind up being nothing to anybody. In trying so hard to be responsible for everything, I failed to become proficient at anything. I tried too hard to live up to the multitude of expectations placed on me instead of focusing on my limited number of gifts and doing the simple things I could do. Somewhere I missed the question Naaman's servants had put to him in the midst of his frustration and anger. I still need to give a daily answer to that question; this chapter is your invitation to make it one of your daily questions.

First, some background. There has never been a

But If Not...

better description of Naaman than this one from the *King James* Translation:

> *Now Naaman, captain of the host of the king of Syria, was a great man with his master, and honorable, because by him the Lord had given deliverance unto Syria; he was also a mighty man of valor, but he was a leper* (II Kings 5:1).

In Naaman's day, a wide variety of skin diseases fell under the heading of leprosy. His was some sort of skin disease that did not create a social barrier, probably some sort of psoriasis. It was severe enough that it created concern even among his servants.

The story begins with an unnamed Israelite maid captured in a raid who finds herself in the service of Naaman's wife. One day she tells her mistress that there is a prophet back in Israel who can heal her husband. Naaman's wife tells him and Naaman tells the king who immediately drafts a letter to the king of Israel instructing him to heal Naaman. Naaman takes the letter along with a gift equivalent to today's quarter of a million dollars and heads for Israel. Jehoram, the king of Israel, is perplexed by both the request and the money. His advisors tell him about the healing prophet Elisha to whom Jehoram immediately sends Naaman.

Wouldn't You Do It?

You would think that if you had leprosy and someone told you how you could be cured, that you would immediately do it. Substitute any dis-ease for the word leprosy and you will find many have the same difficulty Naaman has. A writer tells about a priest he knows who was celebrating mass a few weeks after the sign of peace had been reactivated as a part of the service. After wishing the worshiping community the peace of Christ, he started down the aisle, greeting the people at the end of each pew with a handshake. As he approached one pew, he encountered an elderly woman and offered her his hand. She responded by crossing her arms and hissing, "I don't do that!" The priest said without a pause, "Madam, if you don't shake my hand, I am going to kiss you." Maybe she was acting on the principle of the lesser of two evils, but in any case, her hand flew out, and her lips were spared.[6]

I wish that priest were ubiquitous and could work his miracle on the multitudes who keep themselves apart from community, grace, and healing with the famous words, "I don't do that." These are the words Naaman utters when Elisha's servant comes with the message that the cure for his leprosy is to go and immerse himself seven times in the Jordan River. In furious rage, Naaman announces, "If I had

But If Not...

been into river dousing, I would have done it back home where the rivers are much cleaner. Did I travel all this way to hear this ridiculous prescription for healing?"

Big problem: As with many of us, Naaman wants to prescribe his own cure. He feels slighted that Elisha sends a servant instead of coming himself. Also, he knows that healers work with certain incantations and rituals and the laying on of hands. He knows how healing works. Tragically, he is the one with the leprosy. All he can say is, "I don't do unimportant rivers."

As a professional marriage and family therapist, my wife often encountered troubled couples who poured out their problems and upon hearing the "prescription" for resolution almost shouted in unison, "Oh, we couldn't do that!" And then the couple left in anger because counseling didn't work!

From an email friend, I received these Steven Wright quotes:
  a. Borrow money from pessimists – they don't expect it back.
  b. The early bird gets the worm, but the second mouse gets the cheese.
  c. How do you tell when you're out of invisible ink?
  d. When everything is coming your way, you're in the wrong lane.

e. Hard work pays off in the future, laziness pays off now.
f. I intend to live forever – so far, so good.
g. My mechanic told me, "I couldn't fix your brakes, so I made your horn louder." Unfortunately, I know a lot of people who can't/don't get their problems fixed, they just make their horns louder.

Most of us keep hoping against hope that we can do anything except what needs to be done. We are looking for a magic formula, a secret, an incantation, a great healer, etc. Anything except taking responsibility for our lives and doing what we know is so obviously staring us in the face. Elisha is a prophet with no small reputation. Even though he doesn't come personally to meet Naaman, his prescription is crystal clear. Naaman knows exactly what to do; the problem is, he doesn't want to do it.

Here is where the care and concern of the servants in the household come into play. I find it highly instructive that everybody around Naaman seems to care about him and that his servants even address him as "Father." The servants do not chide Naaman for his anger and rage, they simply point out the obvious: "Hey, nothing else has worked, what have you got to lose? If you go off in a huff you will still have your leprosy. Think about it: if the prophet had asked you to do some very difficult thing, wouldn't you have done it?

But If Not...

Isn't the problem that this seems so simple that you are discounting it? Why not do this very simple thing?"

From an anonymous writer comes this poem titled "Little Things":

> *There is strength in little things;*
> *the snowdrops breaking through the sod,*
> *the echo of the voice of God*
> *in every morning bird that sings.*
> *The balm for spirits crushed and broken*
> *is not made by decree of kings,*
> *but from a thousand little things*
> *like gentle words, like prayers unspoken.*
> *The world is huge; around it rings*
> *the clamor of unending war.*
> *Whatever we are fighting for,*
> *there seems no room for little things.*
> *Yet snowdrops do not cease to grow,*
> *small envoys of successive springs;*
> *the still small voice of little things*
> *brings joy amidst our human woe.*
> *When every day the paper brings*
> *more news of human misery,*
> *Lord, give me strength and grace to be*
> *a voice among your little things.*[7]

Two Prescriptions for Miracles

I am going to suggest two simple things that can bring

real miracles into your life. First, have an eye for the obvious: Don't draw up a "can't do" list, draw up a "can do" list. The simple thing Naaman is to do is to immerse himself seven times in the Jordan River. He may have been persuaded to do it, he may have thought he ought to do it, he may have decided he was going to do it, but until he does it, he isn't healed. It was a simple thing to do – and he does it.

You no doubt have heard what we all need to repeatedly hear: "We are responsible for what we do, no matter how we feel." Our text uses two words to describe Naaman's feelings: *angry* and *rage*. Fortunately, these do not remain his controlling words. Great lesson from The Art of Living 101: Do the simple things you know you ought to do – regardless of how you feel.

> The banner reads "Psychiatric Help 5 Cents"; the sign below indicates "The Doctor is in" and Lucy is ready to listen. "Everything seems hopeless....I'm completely depressed," Charlie Brown begins. Lucy responds, "Go home and eat a jelly bread sandwich folded over...Five cents, please." As Charlie Brown leaves, Lucy informs us, "There are some cures you don't learn in medical school."

Did the jelly sandwich make Charlie Brown feel better? It was something he could do and do for himself. He probably felt better just doing some simple thing – and Lucy no doubt knew that he loved jelly sandwiches. Knowing a thousand things you can't do will bring no benefit. Knowing one thing you can do and doing it can often mean something close to a miracle. And, as is so often the case, it is a simple, obvious thing.

The second suggestion I offer is: Listen for God, Holy Spirit, your Inner Voice, in the common place and the ordinary. I do not doubt that God spoke to Moses out of a burning bush. But I'm not going to hike up a mountain this afternoon looking for blazing shrubbery. I'm going to be "on the listen" for God as I go about the routines of life.

Naaman was quite upset that the great prophet of God, Elisha, did not come out and speak to him directly. I have found that most of the time, messages from God are indirect. In the case of this story, from the prophet's messenger and, before that, from an unnamed servant girl. Learning to be "on the listen" is not easy. Our world is too noisy; it is too full of distractions. I vividly remember driving down Brownsboro Road in Louisville one morning on my way to the office and glancing at the car in the lane next to me. The driver was talking on his cell phone, I could hear the stereo through the open window, and he was reading a newspaper. I quickly got past him.

Be on the listen in unlikely places and with unlikely people. Who would have thought a nameless Israelite servant would have the healing formula for Naaman? The other servants also spoke at the appropriate time words

Naaman needed to hear.

We are not told, but I have often wondered how Naaman felt when he came up out of the Jordan on that seventh plunge? I'm not certain he would have been able to describe what he must have experienced. All because he did some simple thing. As we deal with our own dis-eases, I've often wondered how we would feel if we began to do those simple things we already know we ought to be doing. Those simple things that can make all the difference in the world.

Reflections

In *A Time to Laugh: The Religion of Humor,* Donald Capps gives this story:

> *Upon completing his examination of the patient, the doctor told him to get dressed. "I'm afraid your condition is fairly poor." The doctor sighed. "The best thing for you to do would be to give up liquor, stop smoking, give up all that rich food you've been eating at fancy restaurants, and stop seeing all those young women who keep you out until all hours." The patient thought for a moment. "What's the next best thing?"*[8]

So often in counseling, a client would readily confess knowing what would work best in their situation, but would say something like: "Oh, I know that, but I thought perhaps there was something else I might do." That is the philosophy of the next best thing. Which, of course, is not the best thing – and it may not be quite as simple as Naaman's prescription, but I couldn't close out this chapter without mentioning this aspect of dealing with dis-eases. At least in the above story, the doctor prescribed something that was within the reach of his patient. It was not a "mission impossible."

Any book on problem solving will suggest breaking down big problems into smaller parts and dealing with one part at a time - breaking it down into manageable segments.

But If Not...

Dealing with many of the complex issues of our daily lives begins with the resolution to start with something simple. Cleaning out the attic and garage after being "on the road" for seven years was a monumental task. The solution was to give it thirty minutes a day – that we could do! Will it take a while? Yes! But tackling those two spaces all at once was overwhelming and impossible.

It was not his stated reason for writing the book, but Tom Arnold's *How I Lost Five Pounds In Six Years* has always been my antidote to outrageous claims about almost instant results in dealing with personal challenges. Seven dips in a river will not bring instantaneous healing for any of us – that is not the lesson from this story. The beginning of any healing, transformation, or solution to problems is taking the first steps of doing the simple things that can be done. And, even if not entirely cured or solved, we certainly will find that things are a whole lot better.

---

[1] Peter Gomes, *The Scandalous Gospel of Jesus*, 114.
[2] Robert Collier, *The Secret of the Ages*, 228.
[3] Gregg Levoy, *Callings*, 5.
[4] Bob Sitz, Not Trying Too Hard (Bethesda, The Alban Institute, 2001), 93.
[5] Ibid., 108-109.
[6] Don Kimball, *Power and Presence: A Theology of Relationships* (New York, HarperCollins, 1987), 27.
[7] Ronald Rolheiser, *Against an Infinite Horizon* (New York, Crossroad Publishing Company, 1995), 117.
[8] Donald Capps, *A Time to Laugh* (New York, Continnum, 2005), 25.

Part II: Responsibility, Not Results
Points to Ponder

Would you like to wear the button "Watch out! God loves you!"?

...as God has called you, live up to your calling (Ephesians 4:1).

"Be what you is, not what you ain't, cause if you ain't what you is, you is what you ain't."

It is possible to make a career of fleece tossing.

Does God ever give us a calling that is simply too big for us?

You cannot be anything you want to be and do anything you want to do; you can be what God calls you to be and do what God calls you to do.

Moses didn't know he was Moses until God got through with him.

Duty is ours; events are God's.

What has the philosophy "I don't do that!" kept us from doing? Should we reconsider?

Don't draw up a "can't do list"; draw up a "can do" list.

Be "on the listen" in the ordinary, the daily – both as regards places and people.

Chapter 7: What is God Up To?

MODERN OBSERVATIONS:

> The big idea of this book (An Unsettling God) is that the God of ancient Israel is a God in relationship, who is ready and able to make commitments and who is impinged upon by a variety of "partners" who make a difference in the life of God.[1]

> In Christian theology it might be more appropriate to refer to a return to relationality. Most of the key doctrines that emerged early in the Christian religion are inherently relational; this applies, for example to the uniquely Christian views of God, revelation, and redemption. The doctrine of the Trinity teaches that God is three persons in relation.[2]

> There is no greater challenge for congregations, than becoming a community.[3]

But If Not...

THE BIBLICAL TEXT: II Corinthians 5:19a (*New Living Translation*):

> For God was in Christ, reconciling the world to himself....

A Mountaintop Text

Perhaps the most quoted biblical text during Advent is the line spoken by the angels to the shepherds in Luke 2:10-11: *I am bringing you good news of great joy to all people: to you is born this day in the city of David, a Savior, who is Christ the Lord.*

Questions not fully asked or fully answered are: What does it mean when we are told that Christ has come to be savior? Just what are we saved from and saved to? It is not that most of the answers to these questions are wrong, most are simply too small. Many answers are very small. A series that made its way around was titled "Children's Letters to Santa Claus." Here are two I have in my file:

a. "Dear Santa: Please send me a dog. One that's full of dog. The one I got last year was full of sawdust."
b. Alfred writes: "Dear Santa: Last year you didn't leave me anything good. The year before last you didn't leave me anything good. This year is your last chance."

So much talk about the Incarnation is full of sawdust – it's not real flesh and blood. And if we ever needed something good, it is right now. Many feel it may be our last chance!

If there is a proof text that is also a summary text that pulls into a few words the totality of the biblical witness on the subject of salvation it is II Corinthians 5:19. It tells us

But If Not...

what God was up to in the Incarnation; it tells us what God has always been up to: *God was in Christ, reconciling the world to himself.* This is one of the biblical mountaintops; it provides an excellent viewpoint for lots of things. It provides the perspective needed when dealing with other texts that are not quite as high up the mountain. A good practice in Bible reading and reflection is to mark those passages you consider mountaintops. These are the texts that should receive the most emphasis in your living. I hope you are not shocked when I tell you that not every verse in the Bible is a mountaintop.

Almost everyone has heard the story about President Calvin Coolidge's returning from a Sunday morning worship service and being asked by his wife the subject of the sermon. Coolidge, known for his few words, replied, "Sin." "What did the minister say about it?" his wife enquired further. "He was against it." I can recall at least two people asking me during my interim pastorates when I was going to preach about sin. What they really were asking was when I was going to preach their list of what they considered to be the "worst" sins, assuming that certainly any minister worth his prophetic skills would have the same list.

I have let it be known on more than one occasion during an informal Bible study that I knew what the worst sins were. I would pause, gaze confidently at the group, and announce, "Yours!" That always led to a discussion of just what Paul meant when he wrote: *There is no one who is righteous, not even one....all have sinned and fall short of the glory of God* (Romans 3:10, 23). I always tie that in with Psalm 130:3: *If you, O Lord, should mark iniquities, Lord, who could stand?* I am not the first to insist that while we may be able to avoid certain particular sins, none of us is able to avoid sin. None of us can avoid being a sinner.

I hear very little about the biblical understanding of sin and much about two or three "terrible" sins that should arouse our condemnation and anger (with most of the emphasis on the latter). This takes us back to the Garden of Eden and an analysis of just exactly what went wrong. To read the story at face value, it becomes immediately evident that what happened was a disruption of the relationship Adam and Eve are pictured as having with God. The temptation to which they succumbed is the original one that won't go away: isn't there some way to get control of my life so I won't have to live in "submission" to the Creator? Isn't there some way to declare my independence so that I can get a taste of real life? Isn't God really holding out on me and until I declare my true freedom I'll never get the real blessings that life has to offer?

What happened in that story was the fracturing of the relationship that had been a part of the initial creation. When the narrator tells us that God comes walking through the garden and asking, "Where are you?" he knows exactly where they are. The man and the woman are in hiding; Adam says it is because they are afraid. This is the first mention of fear in the Scriptures; it comes because there is no longer the trust and confidence that came with being in healthy relationship with the Creator. Sin in Genesis 3 has little to do with the nature of the forbidden fruit (not an apple, since apples were unknown in that part of the world), but the fact that Adam and Eve have created an immense fracture in their relationship with God.

This is the reason that the heart of the Gospel message is about the reconciling of the relationship that has been shattered. It cannot be said often enough that it is not God who is out of sorts. He is the one who comes building the bridge back to himself. He doesn't need to be reconciled, we do. While there are no doubt specific sins that all of us have to battle, everything else is secondary to the primary cause of our dilemmas. God's sending his son into the world as savior was all about relationships. The revelation in Jesus Christ is a relational event. It is about bringing together.

When Jesus is asked about the greatest commandment of all, his answer is: *Love the Lord your God with all your heart and with all your soul and with all your mind. This is the first and greatest commandment. And the second is like it: Love your neighbor as yourself* (Matthew 22:36, *New International Version*). Jesus' life and ministry, death and resurrection, were all about bringing people to God and to one another. The purpose of the cross, the purpose of our salvation, is all about creating healthy relationships with God, others, AND ourselves. Once sin can be seen as basically a relational matter, it not only broadens the subject, it speaks to the nature of the necessary remedy.

In the theological model, the basic human problem is not sickness or lawlessness but sin….However we run into it, we run into it as wrecked relationship: with God, with one another, with the whole created order.

The choice to remain in wrecked relationship with God and other human beings is called sin. The choice to enter into the process of repair is called repentance.

The essence of sin is not the violation of laws but the violation of relationships. Punishment is not paramount. Restoration of relationship is paramount, which means that the focus is not on paying debts but on recovering fullness of life.[4]

We All Have Work To Do

My greatest disappointment after so many years in pastoral ministry is how few persons exert genuine effort to enhance the quality of their relationships – or even recognize that this is the first order of business for the church. "Historically, the churches of the Reformation…have focused so sharply on the plan of salvation – soteriology – that they have neglected God's plan for Christian community – ecclesiology."[5] This may be one of the big reasons we find so many people today who announce that they are "spiritual" but not "religious," by which they usually mean not connected with a religious organization. Many have witnessed too many sick, dysfunctional congregations to want to be a part of one.

Whenever I do a workshop on "spirituality," I usually begin with a Sunday morning sermon I call "What Does It Mean To Grow Spiritually?" I contend that the place to begin is at the beginning (not always easily understood!) and I quote Jesus' teaching about the greatest commandment (Jesus brought two commandments together as one). This means the way I measure how I'm doing spiritually, is to keep asking, "Am I growing in healthy and productive ways in my relationship to God, others, and myself?" And you don't leave out any one of these! Then I give the full guideline set forth in II Corinthians 5:17-19:

> *So if anyone is in Christ, there is a new creation: everything old has passed away; see, everything has become new! All this is from God, who reconciled us to himself through Christ, and has given us the ministry of reconciliation; that is, in Christ God was reconciling the world to himself.*

In other words, God is in the bridge-building business. He built the bridge from himself to us and invites us to cross over. The ministry of reconciliation to which we are ALL called means that we are also in the bridge building business.

But If Not...

The question we ask as we examine our attitude and anticipated action is: "Will this help to build a bridge or will it result in bridge destruction?" Not to be forgotten is that we are called to build the bridge whether or not anyone crosses over! What is important is that we have built the bridge; that really solves the dilemma of who goes first in many family and church disputes.

This may be the most difficult area in which to do what we know we ought to do, what we can do, what we are called to do, and let it go. Sometimes reconciliation happens, someone crosses over the bridge we have built – or we meet them in the middle. Sometimes it doesn't happen. What is important is the bridge building, the efforts at reconciliation and redemption.

One of my favorites from a series of children's letters to Santa Claus is this one:

> *Dear Santa Claus, My name is Robert. I am 6 years old. I want a rifle, a pistol, a machine gun, bullets, a hand grenade, dynamite, and tear gas. I am planning a surprise for my big brother. Robert.*

Unfortunately, in our world today that is no surprise! Jesus' mission was to bring people to God and to each other; some are surprised to discover that our mission is the same. Not to be inflammatory, but I take this to be a much larger mission than simply getting as many people as possible into the lifeboats. What our present culture cries out for is a Christian community that shows evidence of true redemption and reconciliation among themselves and demonstrates its willingness to participate as co-reconcilers with God through Jesus Christ.

To my mind, the proof of individual salvation is that it immediately calls us into a community of faith. In Bible studies, I often ask for a reconsideration of the first portion of Scripture as The Old Covenant and the second portion of Scripture as The New Covenant. The first covenant created the community known as Israel; the second covenant created the community known as the church. The creation of community is paramount in both of the covenants. The Model Prayer (The Lord's Prayer) contains the important words *our* and *us*. We pray for God to forgive us as we forgive others. This prayer is a prayer of and for the community. Jesus warns that if when bringing a gift to the altar you remember that a brother or sister *has something against you,* you must: *Leave your gift there before the altar and go; first be reconciled to your brother or sister, and then come and offer your gift* (Matthew 5:23-24). My gifts are to be offered in the context of my community of relationships. There are no "lone ranger" Christians in the New Testament! There are no "I am spiritual" but "not religious" people affirmed in its pages. Our extreme hyper-individualism has totally distorted the central message of Scripture about

But If Not...

God's intention for his creation – to bring us to himself and to one another through Jesus Christ. This only sounds dogmatic because it is!

Of course, living together in community is difficult, challenging, and soul stretching – which it ought to be! I am a human being and only become truly so in relationship to others. Living in relationship (whatever that relationship may be) demands a lot of things: love, patience, understanding, acceptance, humility, compassion, and – most of all – continuing forgiveness. In the Lord's Supper (Communion, Eucharist), when we take the cup, we remember Jesus' words: *This is my blood of the covenant, which is poured out for many for the forgiveness of sins* (Matthew 26:28). There is usually a notation that "other ancient authorities add *new* before the word *covenant*." Paul uses the phrase *new covenant* when writing about the Lord's Supper in I Corinthians 11:25. The new covenant is all about a new relationship with God based solely on grace and forgiveness, God reconciling us to himself, making possible a new relationship. Forgiveness is God's only solution to the "problem" of sin and separation. In the book of Genesis, Joseph and his brothers solve the problems of hatred and hurtful actions the only way they can be solved – with forgiveness. Forgiveness makes a new future possible. It unhooks us from the guilt, shame, resentment and hostility of the past and lets us move ahead.

But If Not...

Martin Luther or John Adams?

Martin Luther and Ulrich Zwingli, prominent Protestant reformers, met with others in October, 1529, in an effort to unify the reform movement. Fourteen points of doctrinal agreement were reached, but they failed to reach an agreement over the meaning of the bread. Zwingli insisted the elements were simply a memorial; Luther insisted on the real corporeal presence of Christ. At the end, with tears in his eyes, Zwingli approached Luther and offered his hand – not the hand of capitulation or compromise, but the hand of community. But Luther declined the overture of Zwingli's outstretched hand and declared, "I am astonished that you wish to consider me your brother," and then the Germans announced to the Swiss: "You do not belong to the communion of the Christian church. We cannot acknowledge you as brethren."[6]

I place this next to the disagreements John Adams and Thomas Jefferson found so severe that they broke off their close friendship. After years of not speaking to one another, a mutual friend persuaded them to write to each other. Adam's letter begins: "You and I ought not to die before we have explained ourselves to each other."[7] Our culture seems extremely short on places and ways to explain ourselves to each other; it is extremely short on places and means of what I call conversation. Too many Christians in their zeal for what they believe to be right, stand with Martin Luther and not with John Adams.

Mark Lowry has a song in which he sings about how he was running late for his flight to Nashville and barely got on the plane. He then continues the story:

> *The flight was over booked and there was someone in my seat. So they took me up to first class where they get real food to eat. I buckled up, we took off, things turned out after all 'til the pilot said, "Welcome to our flight to Omaha!"*

The song is titled "First Class, Wrong Flight." I am often reminded of how often many of us could sing Mark Lowry's song. If we do not see ourselves as first and foremost called to the ministry of reconciliation, we are on the wrong flight – even if everything else we do is first class.

I am deeply saddened at how many well meaning Christians have left behind an unbelievable wake of destruction and alienation as they pursued their cause in defense of God and truth. I have often wished Jesus had elaborated on his charge against the scribes and Pharisees in Matthew 23:15: *"Woe to you, scribes and Pharisees, hypocrites! For you cross sea and land to make a single convert, and you make the new convert twice as much a child of hell as yourselves."* (Most people are not aware that the scribes and Pharisees were NOT the liberals of their day.)

Somewhere a theologian charged that the church has always had a difficult time being as compassionate and loving as their Master. This is strange when it seems so plain that in Jesus Christ God demonstrated once and for all what he has always been up to – the redemption and reclamation of his lost world. Our calling as we live out each day is to be up to the same mission.

Reflections

This was not an easy chapter to write because much of the material is more suitable for workshop discussion. One can quickly be misunderstood when dealing with the mission of the church and how most interpret the meaning of The Great Commission as recorded in Matthew 28:19-20. Too many interpret that verse to mean ONLY what Dwight L. Moody saw as his mission: to get as many people as possible into the lifeboats. In the next chapter I will attempt to unwrap Jesus' conversation with Nicodemus and exactly what it means to be "born again." I repeat: my thesis is that it includes much more than getting in the lifeboat.

Andrew Greely has a chapter in one of his books titled "The Great Parables"; a subsection is titled "Parables As Comedy." Here is a provocative excerpt:

> ...you must ask yourself whether you really believe that God is the kind of God Jesus suggests, a God who is willing to forgive anyone who gives the slightest hint of signing on for the kingdom of heaven, a God who by the standards of human rulers is an easygoing buffoon, a God who expects you to model his forgiveness by forgiving others. A God who, for some godforsaken reason is crazy in love with you.[7]

The only explanation for any of this is that God so loved the world that he gave his son to be the source of redemption and reconciliation. I always tell people that once you come to grips with the absolute miracle of the Incarnation, believing the other miracles is a piece of cake. God's extravagance is what makes possible the reconciliation and bridge building that brings us together. The religious leaders of Jesus' day were quite upset with his unreasonable forgiveness, his unreasonable inclusion of the unfit into the Kingdom of God, and his general unreasonable association with unacceptable people. God's reconciliation and bridge building through Jesus Christ created controversy from the beginning because it did not exclude anyone. That is not only God's continuing purpose, Paul plainly tells us that it is the purpose he has given to each of us. This concept takes a lot of reflection because it has many ramifications.

---

[1] Walter Brueggemann, *An Unsettling God* (Minneapolis, Fortress Press, 2009), xi.

[2] F. LeRon Shults and Steven J. Sandage, *The Faces of Forgiveness* (Grand Rapids, Baker Academics, 2003), 14.

[3] Thomas Edward Frank, *The Soul of the Congregation* (Nashville, Abingdon Press, 2000), 53.

[4] Barbara Brown Taylor, *Speaking of Sin,* 57-59.

[5] Howard Synder, *Decoding the Church,* 79.

[6] C. Douglas Weaver, *From Our Christian Heritage* (Macon, Smyth & Helwys, 1997), 131-132.

[7] Dick Staub, *The Culturally Savvy Christian* (San Francisco, John Wiley & Sons, 2007), xiii.

[8] Andrew Greeley, *Jesus: A Meditation on his Stories and his Relationships with Women* (New York, Tom Doherty Associates, 2007), 135-136.

Chapter 8: Nicodemus Isn't the Only One Who Doesn't Understand

MODERN OBSERVATIONS:

> Bent as we are either on excusing sin or pounding it into the ground, it is no wonder that a third kind of church is so hard to find – not church-as-clinic nor church-as-courtroom, but church-as-community-of-transformation, where members are expected and supported to be about the business of new life. [1]

> ...conversion is not a call to be something other than what we are. Conversion is a call to become more and more of what we are really meant to be. [2]

> " The Beatitudes (Matthew 5:3-12) are not a throwaway list of bedtime benedictions, but the marching orders for a new world."[3]

But If Not...

THE BIBLICAL TEXT: John 3:1-10:

Now there was a man of the Pharisees named Nicodemus, a member of the Jewish ruling council. He came to Jesus at night and said, "Rabbi, we know you are a teacher who has come from God. For no one could perform the miraculous signs you are doing if God were not with him."

In reply Jesus declared, "I tell you the truth, no one can see the kingdom of God unless he is born again." "How can a man be born when he is old?" Nicodemus asked. "Surely he cannot enter a second time into his mother's womb and be born!"

Jesus answered, "I tell you the truth, no one can enter the kingdom of God unless he is born of water and the Spirit. Flesh gives birth to flesh, but the Spirit gives birth to spirit. You should not be surprised at my saying, 'You must be born again.' The wind blows wherever it pleases. You hear its sound, but cannot tell where it comes from or where it is going. So it is with everyone born of the Spirit."

"How can this be?" Nicodemus asked.

"You are Israel's teacher," said Jesus, "and do you not understand these things?"

A Better Translation

It is a much used phrase most of us have heard all our lives. As much as we have heard it you would think it is to be found everywhere in the Bible, but it is only found in the above text and in I Peter 1:23. It is the phrase "born again" that jolted Nicodemus and still jolts many today. Nicodemus is not the only one who does not understand.

From 1993 comes a news article about a bank robber in Minneapolis. He told the arresting police officers that he had been converted at a Billy Graham Crusade and that is why he didn't use a weapon during the holdup. If someone had asked him if he was born again, I'm certain his answer would have been "yes." I pass no judgment, but I think Jesus had a little different meaning in mind.

The importance of what Jesus teaches about being born again is stressed in a way that easily can be missed. The Gospel writer posts a sign that lets us know just how important this teaching is; our translation has taken down this signpost. Our translation reads: *I tell you the truth.* Others translate that phrase as *verily, verily, I say to you* or *truly, truly, I say to you.* In the Greek text it is *amen.* We usually think of this word at the end of something. It means to confirm, to give assent, to add a "so be it" to what has been said or written. Here, Jesus places it at the beginning of what he says; *Amen, amen, I say to you.* As far as I know, there is no Jewish parallel for this. In the Gospel of John, we find this signpost twenty-five times; it comes only from

Jesus. It is found three times in eleven verses in John 3.

Jesus tells Nicodemus: "If you want to be a part of the Kingdom of God (better: the Reign of God), if you want to be a part of God's intention for life in this world, if you want to share in what will one day come to pass on earth as it now comes to pass in heaven, if you want to get on eternity's bandwagon...you've got to be born again."

It is important to note that Jesus lays this demand on one of the best persons in his day. Nicodemus: a trained theologian, one of about 6,000 Pharisees who was dedicated to the keeping of the Law to the smallest detail. He was a good, devout man who came to Jesus at night. Some attack Nicodemus for sneaking in under cover of darkness. However, in that day, evening was the time set aside, after the day's work was done, for busy men to study the Law.[4]

Jesus tells this good man that he MUST be born again. There is no alternative plan. If this demand is laid on all of us (as we believe it is), we certainly need to understand exactly what Jesus is talking about. Translation is never an easy task because it is not a matter of simply substituting one word for another. Jesus spoke Aramaic, the Gospel was written in Greek, and we are reading it in English. Translation difficulties have come back to haunt even the intelligent and knowledgeable. Several years ago, when Pepsi-Cola tried to convert the slogan "Come alive with the Pepsi Generation" into Chinese and German, the effort literally fizzled.

a. In Chinese the message emerged as "Pepsi brings back your dead ancestors."
b. In German it meant: "Come out of the grave with Pepsi."
c. Coca-Cola had similar difficulties advertising in China; the name Coca-Cola in Chinese means "bite the wax tadpole."[5]

When such difficulties occur in a biblical text, it is a far more serious matter. We all know that there frequently can be more than one way to correctly translate a Hebrew or Greek word or phrase; most of the time it doesn't really affect the meaning all that much (but there are exceptions!). In John's Gospel, I believe there is a better way to translate the Greek than *born again*. A footnote in the NIV gives this alternate reading: Or *born from above*. The phrase Jesus uses can be understood in one of two ways: *born again* or *born from above*. On hearing Jesus' words, Nicodemus asks, *"Can one enter a second time into the mother's womb and be born?"* Jesus immediately corrects him: *"You must be born from above."*

Things become much clearer for me when you translate the phrase *born from above*. It makes more sense in verse 8: *"The wind blows where it chooses, and you hear the sound of it, but you do not know where it comes from or where it goes. So it is with everyone who is born of the Spirit."* To be born from above is to be born of the Spirit.

No Easy Matter, No Quick Fix

There are many classic lines in the play and movie *Steel Magnolias*. In one scene, a character who has an especially acid tongue and has just uttered another negative remark is told by one of her friends, "Maybe you need to come to the Mental Health Clinic." The reply is, "I'm not crazy! I've just been in a bad mood for forty years!" That woman needs to be standing with Jesus when he talks with Nicodemus and the wind begins to blow. In both the Hebrew and the Greek, the same word can mean breath, wind, and spirit. The word emphasizes inherent power. The air that people breathed was considered to be the bearer of life. Spirit means power and movement – the power of God, the movement of God. Just as God breathed the breath of life into his creation at the very beginning (Genesis 2:7), so he is able to breathe new life into his creation for a new beginning. It is not unlike being born from above, being born of the Spirit.

This is no easy matter and it is certainly no "quick fix." What Jesus is talking about can never be developed into a formula or reduced to a technique. An author cites a bumper sticker that I, too, have seen: "Christians Aren't Perfect, Just Forgiven." Then he comments: "Just forgiven? And is that really all there is to being a Christian? The gift of eternal life comes down to that? Quite a retreat from living an eternal kind of life now!"[6]

But If Not...

Of course, we know that Christians aren't perfect! (There's too much evidence to the contrary!) Of course, we believe in forgiveness with Jesus as our savior. But Dallas Willard is correct; the bumper sticker does not say enough. It ought to read: "Christians Aren't Perfect, but they are forgiven and committed to letting the Spirit of Christ shape their lives." Too much for a bumper sticker – but so is all good theology.

Another writer tells about a friend of his who met up with a keen Christian woman whose life was a mess. Her marriage was on the rocks, she had had a breakdown, her social life was in ruins and yet when she came to ask for his help she was wearing a sweatshirt that had on it the slogan "Christ is the answer." The counselor took one look at it and said to her, "Jean, I think you should scrap the idea that Christ is the answer. He never said that. He said, 'I am the way.' I think that with him you must seek the answer to your problem."[7]

It is certainly not accidental or incidental that the first designation for early believers was "Followers of the Way." It speaks to something that is at the heart of what we term "conversion." It is a highly corrective way to avoid many distortions. In a reported conversation, a non-believer said, "I am kind of stuck on all this born again talk. So called born again Christians have always turned me off." His friend gave an ingenious reply.

But If Not...

If all that is keeping you from making this leap of faith is words, let's change the words. Instead of calling yourself a born again Christian, substitute something like a BEGUN Christian. It says the same thing. In fact, in this day and age it might even be more helpful.

What bothers you about born-againers is the same thing that sometimes bothers me about them – they seem to give the impression that the new birth means they have finally reached the ultimate in spiritual development. But birth is not an end; it is a beginning, the first halting movements on the road to maturity. If you and I simply call ourselves BEGUN Christians, then we might take seriously the fact that we have a long way to go.[8]

Kathleen Norris writes about "doing the long, hard, tedious work of conversion."[9] I call it being willing to wear the T-shirt that reads: *Under Construction*. Kierkegaard described the task of "becoming" a Christian as opposed to "being" a Christian.[10] Thomas Merton confessed: " My conversion is still going on. Conversion is something that is prolonged over a whole lifetime." Frederick Buechner describes himself this way: "I am not a having-grown-up one but a growing-up one, a groping-one, not even sure much of the time just where my growing and groping are taking me or where they are supposed to take me."[11]

As suddenly as Nicodemus appears in the Gospel of John, just so quickly does he disappear. (It is somewhat unclear where the encounter between Jesus and Nicodemus ends and the commentary of the evangelist begins.) We do find Nicodemus defending Jesus in John 7:50-52 and in 19:38-42 he comes with Joseph of Arimathea to ask Pilate's permission to prepare the body of Jesus for burial. Joseph of Arimathea is termed a "secret disciple" but no such designation appears for Nicodemus. He obviously took seriously what Jesus told him.

The best summary of what is discussed in this chapter (being born from above, born of the Spirit) comes in the suggestion for a church motto. I know of no church that has adopted it but it seems right on target to me. The writer suggests this motto on the board in front of the church: "The Adventure of a Lifetime Begins Here."[12]

But If Not...

Reflections

The question is not asked nearly so much today as it was in times past. Whenever I was asked, "Are you saved?" my response was always: "I was saved, I am being saved, and I will be saved." My concept of salvation is that it is a past, present, and future event. It is ongoing. It is dynamic. In the next two chapters we will discuss some of the ramifications of being born from above (of the Spirit) for daily living. (My thesis: if it doesn't show up there, what evidence is there that it has ever taken place – or, we should say, ever begun?)

Being "born again" has often gotten such a bad rap that I do consider it the appropriate time to reclaim the better translation of being born from above. One of the reasons for the bad press I find in this writer's paragraph about the experience of a friend of his:

> *The needles, the tubes, the beeping chrome monitors, all filled her with horror. Sylvia harbored a paralyzing dread of life-support systems. While visiting a friend in the hospital, however, she determined to bravely steel herself. As she walked through the disinfected corridors, she tried not to peek at the machines in the rooms.*
>
> *It was no use. She needed to get ut.*

Trembling, she reached the nearest elevator and stabbed the down button. When the elevator door opened, a hospital attendant stood beside a gleaming chrome machine covered with tubes and dials. Sylvia hesitated, swallowed, and stepped inside. The door closed. She gazed straight ahead, her face a mask of apprehension. At last she blurted out, "I sure would hate to be hooked up to one of those!" The attendant looked down at the machine and up at Sylvia. "So would I," he said. "It's a rug cleaner."[13]

Far too many believe that being born again is like being hooked up to some terrible system that will be an awful, life-reducing experience. They see it making them narrow and restricted and bigoted. I said a hearty amen aloud to the comment one writer made after hearing a TV minister: "I was amazed by the vastness of his narrowness."[14]

Why cannot we see being born from above as the Spirit of God, the breath of God, the empowerment of God blowing through our lives? First of all, with grace, mercy, forgiveness, love, and acceptance. Then helping us discover those areas/places where we need to grow, develop, and mature in order to become not only what God wants us to become but what we want to become – our best, our real, our true selves.

I believe Nicodemus finally understood this. It certainly makes sense to me.

---

[1] Barbara Brown Taylor, *Speaking of Sin*, 77.

[2] Joan Chittister, *Listen With the Heart* (Lanham, Sheed & Ward, 2003), 28.

[3] Leonard Sweet, *Soul Salsa* (Grand Rapids, Zondervan, 2000), 116.

[4] *The Broadman Bible Commentary,* IX, 240.

[5] Richard Lederer, *The Miracle of Language* (New York, Pocket Books, 1991), 79.

[6] Dallas Willard, *The Divine Conspiracy* (New York, HarperCollins, 1998), 35.

[7] George Carey, *I Believe* (Seattle, Morehouse Publishing, 1991), 48.

[8] James Cox, ed., *Best Sermons 4* (New York, HarperCollins, 1991), 34.

[9] Kathleen Norris, *The Cloister Walk* (New York, Riverhead Books, 1996),323.

[10] Carl Raschke, *The Next Reformation,* 162.

[11] Frederick Buechner, *Secrets in the Dark* (New York, HarperOne, 2006), 206.

[12] Leonard Sweet, *Soul Tsunami* (Grand Rapids, Zondervan, 1999), 198.

[13] Chris Blake, *Searching for a God to Love* (Nampa, Idaho, Pacific Press, 2000), 11.
[14] Ibid, p. 1.

Chapter 9: A Wrestling Match We All Face

MODERN OBSERVATIONS:

We will always be controlled by what we refuse to look at.[1]

"Guilt: the gift that keeps on giving."[2]

We must honor the infinite mystery of our own life's journey to recognize God in it. Or is it the other way around? It seems that God is not going to let us get close unless we bring all of ourselves...including our brokenness. That's why the Good News really is good news. Nothing is wasted.[3]

But If Not...

THE BIBLICAL TEXT: Genesis 32:22-30 (*New Living Translation*):

> But during the night Jacob got up and sent his two wives, two concubines, and eleven sons across the Jabbok River. After they were on the other side, he sent over all his possessions. This left Jacob alone in the camp, and a man came and wrestled with him until dawn. When the man saw that he couldn't win the match, he struck Jacob's hip and knocked it out of joint at the socket. Then the man said, "Let me go, for it is dawn."
>
> But Jacob panted, "I will not let you go until you bless me."
>
> "What is your name," the man asked.
>
> He replied, "Jacob."
>
> "Your name will no longer be Jacob," the man told him. "It is now Israel, because you have struggled with both God and men and have won."
>
> "What is your name?" Jacob asked him.
>
> "Why do you ask?" the man replied. Then he blessed Jacob.
>
> Jacob named the place Peniel – "face of God" – for he said, "I have seen God face to

face, yet my life has been spared."

Reaping What We Sow

I know what he meant, but I think there are more options than the one he gave. It was something said years ago by Fred Allen of old-time radio fame: "Most of us spend the first six days of each week sowing wild oats; then we go to church on Sunday and pray for a crop failure." I have a couple of alternatives when it looks as though I'm about ready to reap a crop of something: "Who put this stuff in my barn? There is no way anything like this could ever be mine!"; or better: "Well, I'll just have to find a way to get this stuff into somebody else's barn."

This is the problem facing Jacob as he returns home. We are not talking about facing the results of six days of sowing wild oats; we are talking about harvesting a crop that has been growing for over twenty years. To change the metaphor a bit – we're talking about the chickens coming home to roost – and the hen house is simply overflowing! Good old Jacob knows he still has a few tricks up his sleeve; little does he know that God has one bigger up his sleeve.

Who is this Jacob we are talking about? This is the Jacob who persuades his brother Esau at a weak moment to sell him his birthright for a bowl of soup. This is the Jacob who, with a little maternal help, tricks his father into giving him the blessing that blind Isaac believes he is giving to his elder son. This is the Jacob who has to flee for his life from his brother's not unexpected wrath and threat to kill him.

Throughout the twenty years of his absence from home Jacob has prospered. This is not surprising because he remains the great schemer and wheeler-dealer. He is returning home loaded with wives, servants, flocks, and wealth. His plan is to send Esau such a lavish gift that the trickery of years past will be forgotten. Messengers are sent ahead with the gifts but Jacob is greatly alarmed when the servants return reporting that Esau is on the way to meet him with four hundred men. Jacob divides his caravan into groups hoping that if they are attacked at least one group will escape.

With his wives and servants sent on ahead, nightfall finds Jacob on the north bank of the Jabbok River near where it empties into the Jordan, about midway between the Sea of Galilee and the Dead Sea. His nightly prayer must have begun with his earlier plea that God save him from Esau. His prayer is: "Deliver me!" Literally, "Snatch me!"(Genesis 32:11). And God says, "No! Let's wrestle!" Before you consider this a three thousand year old out-of-date story, I assure you that it is a wrestling match we all face.

A God-Initiated Wrestling Match

The first thing to note in the Jacob saga is that returning home is not Jacob's idea, it is the result of God's command. An obvious but often ignored lesson in Life 101 is that the only way to deal with our pain is not to go around it or over it or above it or simply to ignore it – we must go through it. Many assume that if certain problems are ignored long enough they will go away. Most counselors (my wife included) contend that when painful difficulties are ignored they usually come back in larger and more destructive forms. Is it tough to face the pain? To walk through the pain? Yes! But it is far tougher to deal with it later on when it becomes a bigger pain.

One counselor writes: "Probably many people I prayed for actually needed to walk into their pain until they realized they were not God."[4] The way we grow, the way we learn, the way we move ahead is to face our pain. God was ready to unveil a future for Jacob he could never have imagined. But, first he had to face the pain of the past – in the person of his brother Esau.

The long ago Art Linkletter "Houseparty" TV show always contained a segment in which children were featured in all their glowing honesty. They were picked by their teachers to appear on the program. Linkletter asked a young lad, "Why did the teacher pick you today?" The boy answered, "Because I have the gift of gab." "Does it ever come in handy?" was the next question. The reply: "Sure! It got me out of school today, didn't it?"

I have always thought he was probably not the only one who was glad it got him out of school that day. He was right; the gift of gab did pay off. He was like Jacob who could talk and trick his way out of almost anything. If he is lucky, the young man will discover one day that you can't talk your way into or out of everything. Not when God says, "Let's wrestle!"

In this strange story (subject to much debate and various interpretations), we discover that Jacob's assailant is God in human form. To be noted is that it is God who takes the initiative. You often hear talk about our wrestling with God, our struggling with God, challenging and questioning his ways, taking God on. You don't hear much about God wrestling with us, God challenging us, God taking us on.

Do you recall the great surprise in the book of Job? Job cries and calls out for an audience with God. He has a lot of questions. When God finally shows up, his opening statement is not, "What are your questions, Job?" but rather, "Job, I've got some questions for you!" That is exactly what God has in mind for Jacob. That is probably what he has in mind for most of us.

What Is The Problem?

Jacob appears to be convinced that his problem, his struggle, is with Esau and everything will come up roses if he can make peace with him. We are aware that Jacob's real problem, his real struggle, is with himself. In this wrestling match, as Jacob comes face to face with God, he comes face to face with his own soul. This wrestling match that God has with Jacob and with all of us, is nothing less than God's taking each of us to the mat in a TV reality show in which we all need to participate – a show called "Let's Face It!"

Jacob is convinced that when he deals successfully with his enemy, his enemy "out there," Esau, all his worries will be over. Jacob has never heard the wisdom of a generation ago uttered down in the swamp in the Pogo comic strip: "We have met the enemy and he is us." (Not unlike the spiritual: "It's not my brother or my sister, but it's me, O Lord, standin' in the need of prayer.")

We are not given any details of this night-long wrestling match. It is my belief that in this unusual encounter with God, Jacob is open and emotionally honest as never before. This is the time for Jacob to face himself and to realize he is a far greater danger to himself than is any threat posed by his brother.

That brings us to a biblical word that has lost much of its original meaning and intention. It is the word with which both John the baptizer and Jesus began their public ministries. It is a word frequently relegated to a one-time initial experience in faith and not placed in the category of one of the on-going necessities in the life of faith. It is the word and the command: "Repent."

Repentance involves a change of mind, a change of direction. It also involves, perhaps even before these two, something much more difficult. "Repentance is not blubbering and self-loathing. Repentance is insight."[5]

At Buzzie's Bar-B-Q in Comfort, Texas, amid the rusty

But If Not...

horseshoes, old six-shooters, beat-up western hats, trophy-deer racks, and the aroma of mesquite-smoked meat, hangs this hand-lettered sign:

> I HAVE GONE OUT TO LOOK FOR MYSELF
> SHOULD I ARRIVE BEFORE I RETURN
> PLEASE HOLD ME UNTIL I GET BACK

Jacob doesn't need to know more about Esau, Jacob needs to know more about himself. He needs genuine insight into himself. Frederick Buechner writes: "Listening to your life is at the top of the hierarchy of human values." The way Jacob makes the greatest discoveries about himself is in his wrestling with God. This is what at least a large portion of our praying should be about – wrestling with God until we come to some truths about ourselves and begin to discover some of our real needs.

What Jacob discovers in his wrestling with God is that he has never felt blessed. He had stolen the blessing from his father that belonged to his brother, but you can't steal a blessing. When the stranger with whom Jacob is wrestling says, "Let me go," Jacob cries out, *"I will not let you go unless you bless me."* Out of this wrestling match Jacob gets a blessing and a great deal more.

Near the end of his life, suffering from illness due in large measure to a lifetime of heavy drinking, a colleague caught W.C. Fields reading the Bible. His friend asked,

"Claude, what in the world are you, an agnostic, doing reading the Bible?" W. C. Fields replied, "Looking for loopholes." I have read this account in several sources, but in a recent one the author offers this suggestion: "Probably, he was looking for grace."[6] I think he was. That's what Jacob is looking for. That's what we're all looking for. We look for it most earnestly when we're up against it, when we've run out of everything else.

The general consensus is that God blesses the worthy, the deserving. If you want to be blessed, you have to get your act together or at least work at being a whole lot better than you are. Or at a minimum, make a promise that you'll be a whole lot better after God blesses you.

I find in Jacob the model for those who are blessed. He is unworthy to receive God's blessing because of his many trickeries: he lied to and deceived his father; he stole from his brother, Esau. (Repeating: blessing can only come as a gift.) After the blessing is bestowed in this episode, Jacob remains an imperfect human being – his limp testifies to that. God blesses the undeserving and flawed, those who know their dark side, their shadow side, their foibles and their weaknesses.

Blessing With A Limp

Jacob gets his blessing, a limp, and a name change. Jacob's antagonist strikes him in the hip socket and it is put out of joint. Most commentators contend Jacob walked with

But If Not...

a limp the remainder of his life. A limp that reminded him of his weaknesses, his vulnerability, his own shortcomings, his own sin, his own limitations, his own unworthiness. When he is asked for his name, he honestly confesses: "Jacob! Heel-grabber, trickster." That name is changed to "Israel" – "one who wrestles with God."

Jacob's ultimate meeting with Esau is one of reunion and reconciliation on a scale Jacob had neither dreamed of or hoped for. It is something he would never have experienced apart from this wrestling match. Jacob walks away with a blessing and a limp. Ironically, never before has he walked so tall or with so much certainty. The end of the story is graphically pictured by the writer in Genesis 32:21: ...*the sun rose above him.*

Who knows? Some time when you are praying, "Deliver me, snatch me away from this," God may simply say, "No, let's wrestle." And you'll never be the same again.

But If Not...

Reflections

Certainly not all restrained or broken relationships will have the same degree of resolution that Jacob experienced with Esau. It is, however, one of the ongoing dilemmas, that, despite Esau's invitation, Jacob settles his family at some distance from his brother. The only other known meeting (Genesis 35:29) is when they participate in the burial of their father, Isaac. An on-going close, personal relationship between the two brothers may have been a little too much to expect.

One of the most unexpected comments from Jacob is this one to Esau: *"...truly to see your face is like seeing the face of God"* (33:10). Not only is God's grace and peace somehow mediated through the face of his brother,[7] but I think that Jacob saw in Esau much that he had never seen before. Forgiveness and reconciliation always enable us to see the other in a new (and better) light. They enable us to see ourselves in a new – and better – light.

Almost all of our worst pain is relational pain. The on-going challenge is to keep asking, "What is in me that has brought this anger, resentment, and estrangement?" For too many, the blame game is the only game in town. That alone never brings insight. It never enables me to bring my best self into attempts at reconciliation.

I have often wondered what God was doing in the life of Esau those twenty years when Jacob was absent? It must have been a great deal. His initial meeting with his estranged brother reminds me of the father of the prodigal (Luke 15:20) who repeats the identical actions of Esau: *And Esau ran to meet him, and embraced him, and fell on his neck and kissed him* (33:4). This is the brother who, twenty years earlier, in his hatred for Jacob had vowed, *"The days of mourning for my father are approaching; then I will kill my brother Jacob"* (27:42). We are never to underestimate what the Spirit may be doing in the lives of those from whom we are estranged. As we give God space in our own lives to work, we must grant the possibility of the same Spirit space in the lives of others.

It is not easy to let go of proscribed responses and expected results to our efforts at reaching out. Relationships remain complex and, frequently, mysterious. Jacob's extravagant gift-bribe was not the cause of Esau's demonstration of brotherly love. God's gift of blessing for Jacob also included this gift of reunion with his brother. Reconciliation does require readiness on our part (whatever that may entail) but we usually confess seeing the hand of God in whatever finally occurs. There is much we cannot do or make happen. Even in forgiveness and reconciliation, letting go is a part of the equation.

"As a psychiatrist, I can always tell when my patients are starting to get better, because they start to increase their connections."[7]

---

[1]Brian Taylor, *Setting the Gospel Free* (London, SCM Press,

1997), 82.

[2]Quoted in Tad Tuleja, *Quirky Quotations* (New York, Galahad Books, 1992), 106.

[3]Richard Rohr, *Near Occasions of Grace, 95.*

[4]Keith Miller, *The Secret Life of the Soul* (Nashville, B & H Publishing, 1997), 197.

[5]Fleming Rutledge, *Not Ashamed of the Gospel,* 336.

[6]Philip Yancey, *What's So Amazing About Grace?* (Grand Rapids, Zondervan, 1997), 35.

[7]F. LeRon Shults and Steven J. Sandage, *The Faces of Forgiveness,* 110.

[8]John Welshons, *When Prayers Aren't Answered* (Navato, CA, New World Library, 2007), 17.

Part III: The Bottom Line: Relationship Points to Ponder

One of the biblical mountaintops is II Corinthians 5:9: *God was in Christ, reconciling the world to himself.*

Sin, before anything else, is a relational term.

The church frequently has focused so sharply on soteriology (the plan of salvation) that it has largely neglected ecclesiology (God's plan for Christian community).

When Nicodemus asks how it is possible to enter a second time into the mother's womb and be born, Jesus corrects him with, *"You must be born from above."*

Jesus never said, "I am the answer." He did say, "I am the way."

Being born from above is the Spirit of God, the breath of God, the empowerment of God blowing through our lives.

To Jacob's plea, "Deliver me!" God responds, "No! Let's wrestle!"

When painful difficulties are ignored they usually come back in larger and more destructive forms.

Pogo's wisdom is timeless: "We have met the enemy and he is us."

Almost all of our worst pain is relational pain.

When the father of the prodigal in Luke 15:20 spots his returning son, he responds just as Esau does when he sees his returning brother (Genesis 33:4).

Part IV: Action! Action! Action!
Chapter 10: Christianity is a Way of Life

MODERN OBSERVATIONS:

Of course faith is very important to Judaism!...What I am saying is that what Judaism precisely rejects as being of little or no value is a faith that does not lead to action.[1]

"An ounce of action is worth a ton of theory."
Friedrich Engels

As Martin Buber teaches, the word of God comes not to be believed in, but to be done.[2]

It is worth noting that the word "Christian" occurs in the New Testament exactly three times and the word "Christianity" exactly zero. The word "disciple," however, is found 263 times.[3]

But If Not...

THE BIBLICAL TEXT: Ephesians 4:17-24; *Revised English Bible*:

Here is my word to you, and I urge it on you in the Lord's name: give up living as pagans do with their futile notions. Their minds are closed, they are alienated from the life that is in God, because ignorance prevails among them and their hearts have grown hard as stone. Dead to all feeling, they have abandoned themselves to vice, and there is no indecency they do not practice. But that is not how you learned Christ. For were you not told about him, were you not as Christians taught the truth as it is in Jesus? Renouncing your former ways of life, you must lay aside the old human nature which, deluded by its desires, is in the process of decay: you must be renewed in mind and spirit, and put on the new nature created in God's likeness, which shows itself in the upright and devout life called for by the truth.

It's Simply Not Biblical

What has bothered me most about it, is that it simply isn't biblical. My concern is reflected in a story that appeared in *The Anglican Digest:*

> *Three rectors got together for coffee one day and found all their churches had bat-infestation problems. "I got so mad," said one, "I took a shotgun and fired at them. It made holes in the ceiling, but did nothing to the bats." "I tried trapping them alive," said the second. "Then I drove 50 miles before releasing them, but they beat me back to the church."*
>
> *"I haven't had any more problems," said the third. "What did you do?" asked the others. "I simply baptized them and presented them for Confirmation," he replied. "I haven't seen them since."*

And, although the traditions vary somewhat, the basic problem is the same. People make a "profession of faith," "get saved," are baptized and more than half of them nobody ever sees again. Although I do believe that the Christian faith begins somewhere, I do believe in conversion and that the term born from above (see the last chapter) is a good term, I do think it is absolutely unbiblical to reduce the Christian faith to an initial "experience" of salvation.

Far too many have believed that the important thing about the Christian faith is to "get saved" and make certain you have a ticket to heaven. After that you can just entertain yourself until the "all aboard" call is given for the express train to Glory. To this, the writer of Ephesians would say: *That is not the way your learned Christ! You were taught to put away your former way of life and to clothe yourselves with the new self created according to the likeness of God in true righteousness and holiness.* In *The Message*, the passage is paraphrased: *You are to take on an entirely new way of life – a God-fashioned life, a life renewed from the inside and working itself into your conduct as God accurately reproduces his character in you.*

Verb Tenses Are Important

Verb tenses in the Greek are often key factors in understanding the meaning of a passage. When the writer (some say not Paul but one of his followers) talks about *laying aside the old human nature* (indicating a change of character), the verb tense indicates a once for all time decision. When we are instructed to *put on the new nature,* the verb tense indicates a continuing process. This understanding lies in back of comments like this one:

I know there are people who say, "My life was

> such a mess. I was drinking, partying, sleeping around...and then I met Jesus and my whole life came together." God bless those people. But me, I had it together. I used to be cool. And then I met Jesus and he wrecked my life. The more I read the gospel, the more it messed me up, turning everything I believed in, valued, and hoped for upside down. I am still recovering from my conversion.[4]

The writer is affirming the process of being renewed in mind and spirit and putting on the new nature created in God's likeness as a challenging and daunting, never-ending process/adventure. In Scripture, when you investigate the meaning of every word having to do with being born from above – salvation, conversion, etc. – you discover that it is never a once upon a time static event but is always a dynamic, continuing process.

With this background, we can begin to understand the way Jesus dealt with those who wanted to be his followers. He reminded them they needed to count the cost, that they would have to deny themselves, take up their own cross, and follow the way he was leading. Many decided there ought to be an easier road to salvation, so they left to find it. On one occasion, so many made a hasty exit that Jesus asked his disciples, *"Will you also go away?"* Their response was, *"Lord, to whom shall we go? You have the words of eternal life"* (John 6:66-68).

In one of his books (unknown location), John Ortberg, a Presbyterian pastor and bestselling author, provides this needed corrective:

> *Imagine an alcoholic going into an AA meeting and hearing, 'We're so glad you're here. We want you to know that you are loved and forgiven through nothing you have done. Of course, we don't expect to change too much. Don't expect to actually stop drinking. We don't like it when people suggest that sobriety is possible. We believe that trying not to drink breeds arrogance and self-sufficiency. We have a little bumper sticker: '12-steppers are not sober, just forgiven.'" Then Ortberg adds this: "The whole point of AA...is to bring freedom from a...power...that was destroying lives."*

The Needed Corrective

The idea of Christianity as a way of life provides the needed corrective for rootless and aimless living. Part of our text is given this paraphrase in *The Message*:

> *And so I insist – and God backs me up on this – that there be no going along with the crowd, the empty-headed, mindless crowd. They've refused for so long to deal with God that they've lost touch not only with God but with reality itself.*[5]

During his teenage years, my younger son frequently used a phrase when we were discussing a matter about which we disagreed. He would finally get to his punch line with, "Get real, Pops!" This was well before the day of our "Reality TV" shows. (Not, of course, my idea of reality.) According to a statistic I recently found, the average adult spends approximately nine hours daily receiving messages from the media. That is sixty-three hours a week compared with the one or two hours the church usually has for communicating the message of the Gospel! No wonder the world has been able to convince us that it knows what reality is all about and can so easily sway those who want to know how to live in a "real" world.

Nancy Mairs confesses: "My family went to church to find God but we did not invite God home with us."[6] We can't afford to yield to this temptation. Not today! Woody Allen was right when he said, "Today we are at a crossroads. One road leads to hopelessness and despair; the other to total extinction. Let us pray we choose wisely."

The Gospel offers us another road, another way. Three quotes point in that direction:

> *"The worst thing that happened to the Christian religion was that it became a religion about Jesus rather than discipleship in the religion of Jesus."*[7]

> *"Churches increasingly became not relational space but propositional space."*[8]

> *"All...inquisitions and holy wars that the church has engaged in over the years are about belief....They don't condemn people for*

living unethically. They condemn them for believing or thinking incorrectly. The problem with emphasizing belief is that it leaves no room for discipleship. Discipleship is the struggle to be like Christ."[9]

And what a struggle it is! My confession is that I have had few problems or struggles with belief. I have had a ton of problems and struggles in trying to be a disciple of Christ. While there are many examples to be cited, one of the things that is most disturbing to me in our day is that the loss of civility is not only a mark of the culture, it is all too often a mark of the people of Christ as well. A current story speaks volumes: A man on a bus stood up to give a woman his seat and she was so surprised, she fainted. When she came round, she said, "Thank you" – and he fainted.[10] Those of us who are his followers ought to be marked by what I call "The Courtesy of Christ." Being courteous does not make one a Christian but surely Christ's people ought to be some of the most courteous people in the world.

A necessary sidebar: I am not ignoring the importance of content in the Gospel. We must have a basis, a foundation, for our faith; doctrine is absolutely essential. What is too often ignored is the logical, necessary, mandatory outgrowth of that doctrine. Paul's letters usually begin with what can be called a doctrinal section. Often this is followed by the word "therefore" (as in Romans 12:1); then Paul gives what is called his ethical section – material dealing with how one lives on the basis of what one believes. Quotes abound that speak to this thesis:

"...when we have to decide which way we are going to bet our entire lives, it is very often our feet that finally tell the tale."[11]

"Being without doing becomes mere image and the management of image....Being with doing teaches us that life is hard, we don't and shouldn't always get our own way, and success has many surprising faces." [12]

"Where is the person who will model for us the beauty of political holiness? Where are the contemplative activists? I will race to their doorways."[13]

Ending With A Crash

When Jesus concludes what we call the Sermon on the Mount, he gives a graphic illustration:

> "Everyone then who hears these words of mine and ACTS on them will be like a wise man who built his house on rock....everyone who hears these words of mine and DOES NOT ACT on them will be like a foolish man who built his house on sand. The rain fell and the floods came, and the winds blew and beat against that house, and it fell – and great was its fall!" (Matthew 7:24, 26-27; Emphasis mine).

The Sermon that begins with *Blessed are* ends with a

tremendous crash! (note the exclamation). The entire sermon could be summarized in three words: "Action! Action! Action!" The putting into practice is everything. The doing is everything. The Sermon is the call to living the Kingdom life in a world that needs the light of those who know what living is all about. It is the Gospel as it is meant to be seen, and not simply heard.

With reasonable assurance of being misunderstood, I conclude this chapter with a quote from Rabbi David Rosen: "A more appropriate word to describe what is called *Orthodoxy* (meaning "correct belief") is *Orthopraxis* (meaning "correct behavior").[14]

But If Not...
Reflections

Bob Sitze provides many helpful (and often surprising) insights in his book *Not Trying Too Hard*. In a section titled "How change occurs," he writes: "Change starts with behaviors, not ideas. Because you 'act your way into thinking,' changed behaviors may be the first step in a process of change, instead of the last step."[15] This is a sound psychological principle that undergirds the biblical mandate to action. (A little more about this in the next chapter.)

For years in Bible studies, I would use the phrase: "We don't feel our way into new actions, we act our way into new feelings." Attitudes are changed as we act in new ways. To develop a new attitude we need to develop a new pattern of behavior. Another way to come at this issue is: we may not be able to help the way we feel, but we can help the way we act. When Jesus commanded us to love our enemies, he was not talking about attempting to develop a warm feeling toward those who are attempting to do us harm. He was talking about the positive and constructive actions that do not bring harm to the other. In time, we may discover that our attitude is changing.

In his new commandment (often called the Eleventh Commandment) that we love one another as he loves us (John 15:12), he is not commanding our attitude but our behavior. He is not commanding our feelings, he is issuing a command about the way we are to act. I Corinthians 13 (Paul's famous "love" chapter) describes love, not as an emotion, but as behavior. Repeating: we may not be able to choose our feelings but we can choose our actions. C. S. Lewis was not endorsing a hypocritical stance when he wrote: "Do not waste time bothering whether you 'love' your neighbor; act as if you did."[16]

If further proof is needed that you act your way into new thinking, it comes from recent studies indicating that "significant events in your life, including significant choices you make about how you behave, create new information pathways and patterns within your brain….Parts of the brain actually become physically enlarged when an individual's behavior regularly exercises them."[17] A good credo for the Christian life remains: "Action! Action! Action!"

R. T. Kendall and David Rosen, *The Christian and the Pharisee* (New York, Faith Words, 2006), 63.

[2] Rachel Mikva, ed., *Broken Tablets: Restoring the Ten Commandments and Ourselves* (Woodstock, Jewish Lights Publishing, 1999), xviii.

[3] Brian McLaren, *A New Kind of Christianity* (New York, HarperOne, 2010), 28-29.

[4] Shane Claiborne, *The Irresistible Revolution* (Grand Rapids, Zondervan, 2006), 41.

[5] Eugene Peterson, *The Message* (Colorado Springs, Navpress, 2002).

[6] Nancy Meirs, *Ordinary Time* (Boston, Beacon Press, 1993), 106.

[7] Walter Shurden, ed., *Proclaiming the Baptist Vision: The Priesthood of All Believers* (Macon, Smyth & Helwys Publishing, 1993), 131.

⁸Leonard Sweet, *The Gospel According to Starbucks* (Colorado Springs, Waterbrook Press, 2007), 131.
⁹Ibid.
¹⁰Bob Monkhouse, *Just Say A Few Words* (New York, Virgin Books, 2004), 122.
¹¹Frederick Buechner, *Secrets in the Dark*, 45.
¹²Richard Rohr, *Near Occasions of Grace*, 16.
¹³Ibid
¹⁴R. T. Kendall and David Rosen, *The Christian and the Pharisee*, 111.
¹⁵Bob Sitze, *Not Trying Too Hard*, 233.
¹⁶C. S. Lewis, *The Inspirational Writings of C.S. Lewis* (New York, Inspiration Press, 1987), 37.
¹⁷N. T. Wright, *After You Believe* (New York, HarperOne, 2010), 37.

Chapter 11: Right Here! Right Now!

MODERN OBSERVATIONS:

"One of the illusions of life is that the present hour is not the critical decisive hour."
   - Ralph Waldo Emerson

"I care not for a man's religion whose dog and cat are not the better for it."
   - Abraham Lincoln.

"The best thing about the future is that it comes one day at a time."
   - Abraham Lincoln.

But If Not...

THE BIBLICAL TEXT: Matthew 24:45-51; *Revised English Bible*:

> *Who is the faithful servant, charged by his master to manage his household and supply them with food at the proper time? Happy that servant if his master comes home and finds him at work! Truly I tell you: he will be put in charge of all his master's property. But if he is a bad servant and says to himself, "The master is a long time coming," and begins to bully the other servants and to eat and drink with his drunken friends, then the master will arrive on a day when the servant does not expect him, at a time he has not been told. He will cut him in pieces and assign him a place with the hypocrites, where there is wailing and grinding of teeth.*

Questions, Questions, Questions

Recently, someone said to me, "Now with many years of pastoral experience under your belt, I bet you have better answers than when you started out." I responded, "Not necessarily. But I do have better questions." The importance of better questions has been underscored by many:

A university president: "The quality of our lives is determined, first of all not by the kind of answers we propose but by the kind of questions we ask."[1]

And from Voltaire: "Judge persons by their questions rather than by their answers."

In the above text, Jesus asks one of the most important questions that those of us as individuals and members of a particular congregation need to hear: *Who is the faithful and wise servant?* And then he proceeds to give us the method by which we might answer that question.

This question has always been important. In the context of our culture and world, it seems to me more important than ever. The first phrase I think of in attempting to describe our present circumstances comes from Marc Connelly's play from another time, *Green Pastures*. Based on the story of Noah and the flood, the classic line describing the world before the deluge is: "Everything nailed down is coming loose." One of the ways to describe that today has been coined in the phrase "change toxicity."[2] Tied into that,

But If Not...

of course, is the definitely postmodern dis-ease of "information overload."

Instead of lessons in hand wringing and screaming from opened windows, "We are mad as (you know what) and won't take it any longer!" we need to listen to some insightful and prophetic voices. Like the voice of Wendell Berry and his analysis in *Standing by Words* in which he draws the distinction between *public* and *community*. A summary of his thought is that the term *public* means people abstracted from the personal responsibility of belonging. Thus, a public building is one that belongs to everyone, but to no one in particular. In contrast, a community has to do first of all with belonging. It is a group of people who belong to one another and to their place.[3]

When you read Paul's letters in the New Testament, you find they are to specific congregations in specific places. Paul encourages these congregations to live out the Gospel fully right where they are, just as they are.

I have seen the catch phrase on coffee mugs: "If not now, when?" I would add another phrase: "If not here, where?" Meaning in the context of this chapter: Today, on the basis of who I am, where I am, and the gifts I have, what can I do as a faithful follower of the one I call Lord?" Hence, the chapter title: "Right Here! Right Now!" Putting these verses in the larger context gives us a better understanding of how to do this. We need the constant reminder that none of the Bible was written in chapters and verses. Matthew's gospel is best understood when read (or even better, heard) as one seamless work.

The Lesson for the Day

The section of material that provides the larger context for 24:45-51 begins with the question from the disciples about the end of the age. The major thrust of Jesus' response is that a date cannot be known but what is important is: *Keep awake!* (25:13). Plain translation: *Remain faithful.* After the words *keep awake*, Jesus tells the parable in 24:45-51. *Keep awake* is repeated in the parable of the five foolish and five wise bridesmaids. Following that is the story of the three servants entrusted with funds to invest while the master is away (the famous parable of the talents). The final parable is about separating the sheep from the goats and those who feed the hungry, give water to the thirsty, provide shelter for the homeless, and visit those who are in prison. (Please note: this is Jesus' list, not mine!). The conclusion is the grand finale proclamation: *Truly I tell you* (or *Amen I tell you), just as you did it to one of the least of these...you did it to me* (Matthew 25:40).

It is all summarized in our initial text where Jesus defines the faithful and wise servant as the one whom his master finds AT WORK when he returns. (Jesus answers the question he asks.) At work – right where we are, doing what we can do, with the gifts we have. Even if that means *least, small, insignificant*. We are into such comparisons that we often lose sight of what we are called to do. We need to read frequently the episode at the end of John's gospel where Peter is given his charge of what he is to do. He then looks over at another disciple and asks Jesus, *"What about him?"* Jesus' curt reply is: *"...what is that to you? Follow me"* (John 21:21-22, *Revised English Bible*). Peter's problem is reflected in the problem of the unfaithful steward in the parable of the talents who digs a hole and buries his giftedness because his talent in only single-digit in comparison to the double-digit and five-digit gifts of the other two servants. "What can I do?" so often results from looking around with comparative (and envious) eyes.

Incidentally, I don't find anywhere that Paul writes to a church and says, "Your problem is you're not growing." Any negative judgment is usually, "You're not being faithful to your calling." I have often wanted to hear (not having the courage to preach it myself) a sermon based on the occasion in the gospels when Jesus looks at a huge throng assembled to hear him and announces to his disciples, "This crowd is too big!" Most of us success-oriented ministers would choke on that! One writer charges that with all our emphasis on church growth, many congregations have lost touch with their soul.[4] Perhaps it is time to see the beauty of small things. Time to remember Jesus' word *least* as the challenge to stop thinking about size or seeming significance. This is a good time to remember the work of Mother Teresa who labored with a group in Calcutta for forty years ministering to those whom others simply left on the streets to die. Her watchword was: "We are not called to be successful. We are called to be faithful." She would not allow anyone to define success for her. Her stance was correct. Only the Lord will give the final declaration about who and what was truly successful. All biblical indications are that it will not be unlike the Gomer Pyle announcement: "Surprise! Surprise! Surprise!" Surprise as to who's first and who's last and who's in and who's out.

The thesis of faithfulness: We do what we feel called to do, what we know we ought to do, what we can do right here and right now with the gifts that belong to us. That's it. In Christian service, you don't begin with the question, "How will this turn out?" You start with the question, "What is that I can and should be doing."

There is popular adage around, "Do what you love and the money will follow." The best challenge to that philosophy is the career of Vincent van Gogh. His paintings today are worth millions; the money did follow, but not to him. Perhaps the greatest challenge in life is to do what you love to do, what you have a passion to do, what you feel called to do – regardless of how things turn out. Do it and let it go." These six words cannot be repeated often enough. If there is any formula for peace, any "secret" of peace, this is it.

Already mentioned is Bob Sitze's *Not Trying Too Hard*. The subtitle is *New Basics for Sustainable Congregations*. It is not only about how to maintain a healthy church, it is also about how to maintain a healthy life, period. One of my favorite lines from the book is: "You start and end your daily activities with the assurance of grace."[5] This is the assurance of being fully accepted, loved, and called just as you are – doing what you can do in the context of your concrete situation, circumstances, and limitations.

The bottom line: The time to hope, live, and invest fully in whatever your calling, is right here, right now!

Reflections

Unable to find the word in a dictionary, I thought my boyhood pastor had made it up. He often underscored the need for "spizzerinctum." I had almost forgotten the word until I found it in Leonard Sweet's *The Gospel According to Starbucks*: "Spizzerinctum involves the habit of saying yes to the moment."[7] This underscores the tradition called "The Sacrament of the Present Moment." A contemporary version of the same idea is Eckhart Tolle's *The Power of Now*.

We will deal with this concept later in the final section, but it is obvious to me that achieving "Right here! Right now!" calls for what Paul Jones terms "the discipline of focused immediacy." In that focus, the "eye is cleansed and freshened by dropping the scales of inattention."[6] It is widely accepted that we live in the postmodern era (whatever that means is also widely debated). A better description of our times might be "the age of distraction." We are so busy paying attention to everything that we actually are paying attention to nothing.

The key to understanding the burning bush episode in Exodus is contained in 3:4: *When the Lord saw that (Moses) had turned aside to see, God called to him out of the bush, "Moses, Moses!"* Moses possessed "the discipline of focused immediacy" and thereby found (heard) his calling. "Does not pay attention" was one of the phrases often

But If Not...

included on report cards issued by elementary teachers when I was going to school. Why learning to pay attention should be one of the "secrets" to successful living, successful relationships, remains a mystery to me This is not to say that I still do not find it difficult to accomplish! I continue to pursue that discipline!

To be faithful, one must be awake. To be faithful one must be present in the place and time where one is standing. An Amish farmer in Pennsylvania is reported to have issued the challenge: "Remember the importance of small things done at the right time." At the beginning of each day, discarding the "Can't do list" and drawing up a "Can do list" is one way to achieve this. Recovering the beauty of small things done at the right time is one of the roads to genuine transformation. It certainly is the way out of the "only one talent" syndrome. Being a faithful servant "at work" begins with getting into the action mode with whatever we know our task (job) to be. I continue to review my daily calendar and draw up a list. It is a very simple list titled, "This is what I will do TODAY." That means, right here, right now. It's the only place I have. It's the only time I have.

---

[1] Kirby Godsey, *Centering Our Souls* (Macon, Mercer University Press, 2005), 6.
[2] Bob Sitz, *Not Trying Too Hard,* 10.
[3] Joel Shuman and Roger Owens, eds., *Wendell Berry and*

Religion (Lexington, University of Kentucky Press, 2009), 22.
[4]Thomas Frank, *The Soul of the Congregation,* 21.
[5]Bob Sitz, *Not Trying Too Hard,* 207.
[6]W. Paul Jones, *Trumpet at Full Moon,* 135
[7]Leonard Sweet, *The Gospel According to Starbucks*, 86.

Chapter 12: I Believe in Maturity, Not Perfection

MODERN OBSERVATIONS:

Groucho Marx: "How long have you been married?" Woman: "Three wonderful years." Groucho: "Never mind the wonderful years. How many miserable years have you had?"
(From the TV series You Bet Your Life.)

The poet Rilke reminds us that the purpose of life is to be defeated by greater and greater things.[1]

I don't find in the New Testament any suggestion that the visible church ought to be composed of guaranteed 100 percent soundly converted keen Christians. If it had been, half the epistles would not have been necessary.[2]

THE BIBLICAL TEXT: Matthew 5:45-48:

You have heard that it was said, "Love your neighbor and hate your enemy." But I say to you, Love your enemies and pray for those who persecute you, so that you may be children of your Father in heaven; for he makes his sun rise on the evil and on the good, and sends rain on the righteous and on the unrighteous. For if you love those who love you, what reward have you? Do not even the tax collectors do the same? And if you greet only your brothers and sisters, what more are you doing than others? Do not even the Gentiles do the same? Be perfect, therefore, as your heavenly father is perfect.

But If Not...

Imperfection Is Here To Stay

Perfection is not a biblical idea. In the above text, the English word *perfect* translates a Greek word rich in meaning. A clearer translation is: *Therefore...you shall be those who are complete in your character, even as your Father in heaven is complete in His being.*[3] The single Greek word translated *perfect* contains within it the basic themes of wholeness, completeness, maturity, and purpose. The call in this passage is for maturity, not perfection.

I almost wanted to make my first point: "Let's Hear It For Imperfection!" but I toned it down to "Imperfection Is Here To Stay!" Over a decade ago, I purchased a book titled *The Spirituality of Imperfection*. Recently, I attended the Annual Clergy Conference sponsored by a hospital. The topic for the session was *The Spirituality of Imperfection*; the session focused on this factor as a key ingredient in good emotional and physical health and always a needed aspect in ministry. A fourth-century monk, Marcarius, wrote: "All improvement in spirituality is a matter of falling and getting up again, building something up and then being knocked down again."[4]

John Wesley maintained that it is impossible to hold a conversation lasting more than thirty minutes without saying something that shouldn't be said.[5] Most of us discovered this truth on our own without knowing about Wesley's warning. I would often include this reminder in a service of deacon ordination: "You are not being ordained to perfection."

But If Not...

Why people outside the church are surprised that people inside the church are human beings is still a mystery to me. None of us has lost our humanity. We may be "saved" sinners but we remain sinners – meaning we continue to miss the mark and fall short of the glory God intends in our lives. There are many ways this has been stated but none better than from Anne Lamott who quotes a friend who is a recovering alcoholic. She said that when she'd gotten sober, she saw that even though you get the monkey off your back, the circus never really leaves town.[6]

David Roche uses humor to communicate the same message. He invites all of us (through his book and personal appearances) to participate in a church that suits all of us for exactly where we are. He calls it the Church of Eighty Percent Sincerity. "Eighty percent is about as good as it's going to get... So twenty percent of the time you get to be yourself."[7]

He talks about unconditional love which he acknowledges as a reality but that has a shelf life of about eight seconds. Instead of beating ourselves up because we feel it so fleetingly, we should savor the moment when it appears. As David puts it, "We might say to our beloved: 'Honey, I've been having these feelings of unconditional love for you for the last eight to ten seconds.' Or, 'Darling, I'll love you unconditionally till the very end of dinner.'"[8] Only God can always have unconditional love. The rest of us continue to try to attain it in our incomplete ways. That's the way it will always be. Because we are human.

But If Not...

I read about one person's spiritual journey and the time (real or imagined?) he went to see his spiritual guide and found himself in front of a building called The Tower of Therapy. As he was about to knock on the door, he noticed a posted sign hanging on the wall to his left. He took a step back to focus on the message:

> *Welcome. If you're early, you're anxious, if you're on time you're compulsive, if you're late you're resisting. You can't win. Winning, however, is not the point. The point is to stop hiding from and lying to yourself.*[9]

The spirituality of imperfection is this acknowledgment. It's the call to be real. It seems to me that in the Gospels, Jesus was attracted to and affirmed people who were real. His major problems were with the most religious people in his day whom he called "actors" (the meaning of the word *hypocrite*). You can relate to people who are real. It is very difficult to relate to those who are playing a part and wearing a mask (another characteristic of actors in that day).

Martin Luther evidently had a major problem with his colleague, Philip Melancthon, who was quiet and virtuous to an extreme. He reportedly said to him one day, "For goodness sake, why don't you go out and sin a little? Doesn't God deserve to have something to forgive you for?"

It is difficult to relate to people who are constantly

But If Not...

parading their virtues and almost impossible to relate to those who are perfect (as least, in their own eyes). Communities are usually not constituted around virtues; it is our shared common weaknesses that provide the cement for togetherness. We need look no further than AA to affirm this principle. No one is permitted to begin addressing the group without this introduction, "My name is _____ and I'm an alcoholic." This remains the opening even if the person has been sober for years.

Maturity: A Pursuit, Not an Achievement

If we are not called to be perfect, what does it mean to be called to be mature? In the context of Matthew 5:48 it is fairly plain. Jesus says that we are to be complete in our love just as God is: God sends rain on the just and the unjust. God loves on the basis of who he is and not on the basis of what someone deserves. Jesus calls us to be so centered and focused that our responses to others can always be based on who we are and what we are about and not on the misconduct or mis-action of another.

We don't have many models today on how to relate to those who disagree with us, those who have other opinions, see things another way, or sometimes those we would classify as enemies. The maturity Jesus wants us to have is the perfection of his Father who is not thrown off course by anything anyone in his creation ever does. He asks all of his followers: *What more are you doing than others?* Or as in the William Beck Translation: *Are you doing anything extraordinary?*

Albert Einstein, at a time when he was already white-haired, was reportedly sitting next to an eighteen-year old at a dinner party. When the conversation flagged, the young lady asked him, "What are you actually by profession?" Einstein quietly replied, "I devote myself to the study of physics." She retorted in surprise, "You mean to say you study physics at your age? Why, I finished mine years ago."

My major reason for not liking the question "Are you saved?" is because it implies that salvation is a transaction – a completed transaction. (See Chapter 8 for a fuller discussion.) The better question for me is, "Have you begun your faith journey as a disciple of Jesus Christ?"

Ninety-one year old Pablo Casals was performing his daily routine of cello practice when a student asked him, "Master, why do you continue to practice?" Casals answered, "Because I'm making progress." What is important in the faith journey is not where you are but that you are making progress. There is no better conclusion for this chapter than these words from Reinhold Niebuhr:

> *Nothing that is worth doing can be achieved in our lifetime; therefore, we must be saved by hope. Nothing which is true, or beautiful, or good, makes complete sense in any immediate context of history; therefore, we must be saved by faith. Nothing we do, however virtuous, could be accomplished alone; therefore, we must be saved by love.*

But If Not...

No virtuous act is quite as virtuous from the standpoint of our friend or foe as it is from our own standpoint; therefore, we must be saved by the final form of love, which is forgiveness.[10]

But If Not...

Reflections

I was introduced to Joan Chittister almost a decade ago at a conference in which she was one of three featured speakers. All were excellent but, as we often say, she stole the show. That conference led me to the purchase of several of her books that I have found to be invaluable resources in my spiritual journey. From her I learned that the Talmud teaches that every human being should wear a jacket with two pockets. In one, the rabbis say, we should carry the message, "I am a worm, and not even fully human." In the other, should be the message, "For me the world was made."[11]

This is only one of the many inescapable paradoxes that one discovers over the course of the life-journey. "All or nothing" is the exception, not the rule, for most of our life-encounters. I was once accused of doing something with a "mixed-motive." My accuser was taken aback with my response, "All of my motives are mixed." That was not a word of boasting but a word of confession. My aim may be to move toward more pure motives in my actions but I will never reach 100%. "Maturity, not perfection," makes peace with our common humanity while challenging us to "keep on the grow."

Most of us need to replace the word "criticism" with the word "evaluation." The first still has the connotation of something that is hurtful and negative; the second speaks to analysis and means of improvement. Coming to the place where we can say, "It would have been more helpful if I had..." instead of "I was so stupid!" is a quantum leap in self-evaluation. One encourages feed-back while the other tends to keep us in the defensive mode. Condemnation, while easy and sometimes just loads of fun, has never been a liberating word. If that is our only word in a given situation, either for ourselves or for others, hope takes a holiday. Many of Jesus' harshest critics couldn't understand how he could offer forgiving and liberating words to those whose conduct clearly called for severe judgment. I don't think you can make any kind of a case for Jesus being "soft on sin." He never bypassed the hurt and destruction brought about by those actions that missed the mark of what God intended for human relationships. What Jesus offered was not, "Oh, what you did doesn't really matter. It's okay. After all, we're all only human."

In his presence, others came to see themselves all too clearly for who they were. I have often thought their experience must have been like that of Isaiah's Temple experience in Isaiah 6. When confronted with the holiness of God (and not a spoken word of judgment against him), his immediate response is to cry out, *"Woe is me! I am lost, for I am a man of unclean lips, and I live among a people of unclean lips; yet my eyes have seen the King, the Lord of hosts!"* There is immediately a divine-initiated cleansing ceremony with the announcement: *"...your guilt has departed and you sin is blotted out"* (6:7). Isaiah is then ready to respond to his unique prophetic call. In the same way, those who encountered the glory and grace of God in Jesus, did not depart with "Woe is me!" as their life motto. From him they received the liberating words of forgiveness that enabled them to embrace life – fully and imperfectly.

---

[1] Gregg Levoy, *Callings*, 266.
[2] N. T. Wright, *Small Faith, Great God* (Downers Grove, Illinois, IVP Books, 2010), 142.
[3] Kenneth Wuest, *The New Testament, An Expanded Translation* (Grand Rapids, Eerdmans, 1998).
[4] Ernest Kurtz, *The Spirituality of Imperfection* (New York, Bantam Books, 1994), 134.
[5] Leonard Sweet, *Out of the Question...Into the Mystery* (Colorado Springs, WaterBrook Press, 2004), 143.
[6] Anne Lamott, *Grace Eventually* (New York, Riverhead Books, 2007), 252.
[7] Anne Lamott, *Plan B* (New York, Riverhead Books, 2005), 109.
[8] Ibid.
[9] John Powers, *And Grace Will Lead Me Home* (New York, McCracken Press, 1994), 44.
[10] Krista Tippett, *Speaking of Faith,* 225.
[11] Joan Chittister, *In Search of Belief* (Liguori, Missouri, Liguori/Triumph, 1999), 45.

But If Not...
Part IV: Action! Action! Action!
Points to Ponder

Being renewed in mind and spirit is a challenging, daunting, and never-ending process/adventure.

The idea of Christianity as a way of life provides the needed corrective for rootless and aimless living.

Being courteous does not make one a Christian, but surely Christ's people ought to be some of the most courteous people in the world.

The Sermon on the Mount doesn't end with an "Amen" but with a crash.

We don't feel our way into new actions, we act our way into new feelings.

If not now, when? If not here, where?

Paul does not criticize churches for not growing; he criticizes them for not being faithful to their calling.

Perhaps it is time to see the beauty of small things.

Spizzerinctum involves the habit of saying yes to the

moment.

Human perfection is not a biblical idea, that is reserved for God alone.

Even though you get the monkey off your back, the circus never really leaves town.

Part V: On Being Inner-Directed
Chapter 13: The Amazing Power At Work In Us

MODERN OBSERVATIONS:

This pilgrimage of spirit with Spirit is what we mean by "spirituality."[1]

Advent and Lent celebrate "God with us." Christmas and Easter celebrate "God for us." Epiphany and Pentecost celebrate "God in us."[2]

Gibbon's annihilating comment on the whirling dervishes of the desert: "They mistook the giddiness of the head for the illumination of the Spirit."[3]

THE BIBLICAL TEXT: Ephesians 3:16-21:

I pray that, according to the riches of his glory, he may grant that you may be strengthened in your inner being with power through his Spirit, and that Christ may dwell in your hearts through faith, as you are being rooted and grounded in love. I pray that you may have the power to comprehend, with all the saints, what is the breadth and length and height and depth, and to know the love of Christ that surpasses knowledge, so that you may be filled with all the fullness of God.

Now to him who by the power at work within us is able to accomplish abundantly far more than all we can ask or imagine, to him be glory in the church and in Christ Jesus to all generations, forever and forever. Amen.

But If Not...

For All Us Ordinary Folk

There seems to be an unspoken assumption that the really great parts of the Bible are for super saints or those who give their full time to religious matters. One of the reasons we can read a passage like Ephesians 3:16f. and not feel the thrill of incredible possibilities is that somehow we have concluded it is not for the "average" believer (whoever and whatever that is). When Paul writes this letter to the church at Ephesus, he writes to ALL, to "ordinary" people who have all the good qualities and weaknesses of church members in any time and any place.

How many of us take seriously such loaded words in the text like: *according to the riches of his glory; you may be strengthened in your inner being; now to him who by the power at work within us is able to accomplish abundantly far more than we can ask or imagine.* (Literally the word translated *abundantly* is: *superabundantly beyond and above).*

A member was once asked how she liked the new minister who had recently come to be pastor. She replied, "He is wonderful! You know what? Our new minister asks God for things our former minister didn't even know God had!" Do we really believe God has all Paul says he has: Riches of his glory to share with us? The ability to strengthen us in our inner being? Power at work in us to accomplish abundantly far more than we can ask or imagine?

Defining the Power

We are talking about that which is not simply inspiration but something that is the energizer of our lives. We are talking about the amazing power at work in us. Two questions need to be asked: First, what is this power? Second, why aren't more believers aware of and responsive to the amazing power at work within them?

It seems a tragedy to me that many Christians stopped believing in something that secular books on spirituality have never stopped emphasizing. These books use phrases like: "The God within." "The divine spark in all of us." They mean getting in touch with the very center of our beings, the center that is more than the sum of the material world, the spiritual in our lives. This is spirituality in the generic sense.

When Paul writes about the power at work in us, he is writing about something specific. Too many are like those Paul met in Acts 19: *Paul passed through the interior regions and came to Ephesus, where he found some disciples. He said to them, "Did you receive the Holy Spirit when you became believers?" They replied, "No, we have not even heard that there is a Holy Spirit."* We may not fall into this category, but there is the persistent understanding that Holy Spirit belongs only to groups that characterize themselves as "charismatic."

In my first church after being graduated from seminary, I expected a whole lot more enthusiasm than I found. I learned that it is possible for BOTH congregation and pastor to have unrealistic expectations. On an especially lifeless Sunday morning, during my sermon I paused and quietly asked, "How long has it been since you have felt the presence of the Holy Spirit?" After the service, one of the deacons put an arm around my shoulder and said, "Now, pastor, don't be too discouraged. A lot of ministers better than you have tried to change us and they couldn't do a whole lot." He meant this as an encouraging word.

It's probably good that I didn't know then when I know now or I might have punched holes in the ceiling of the sanctuary. In tenth century Rome, on Pentecost Sunday, the mystery of the Spirit was dramatized. There were "Holy Spirit holes" in the ceilings of the churches, opening them to the sky, dramatizing architecturally the openness of the church to God and the fact that the Spirit cannot be contained within the church. Also, doves were let loose through these holes to fly about in the church and bundles of rose petals were released to fall down on the people like tongues of fire (Acts 2:3).[4]

When we understand the terms, we find that we need enthusiasm far more than we need inspiration. The word *enthusiasm* is from the Greek and means "filled with God." Enthusiasm has to do with our inner beings, the very heart and soul of life, the inner workings of who we are. The scriptures teach that the source of this enthusiasm is within each of us.

But If Not...

Jesus promised his disciples that he would not leave them orphans, he would not abandon them. He promised that they and all future disciples would be the recipients of Holy Spirit, the Spirit of God, his Spirit. A major sidebar: "It is clear in the New Testament that the Spirit is a gift, not a reward."[5] A gift to EVERY believer. Many need to hear the words Paul found it necessary to write to a church generations ago (I Corinthians 6:19): *...do you not know that your body is a temple of the Holy Spirit within you, which you have from God...?*

The answer to our first question, what is this power? The amazing power within you is the Spirit of the living God.

Accessing This Power

The answer to our second question begins with two warnings:

> (Ephesians 4:30-32):....*do not grieve the Holy Spirit of God, with which you were marked with a seal for the day of redemption. Put away from you all bitterness and wrath and anger and wrangling and slander, together with all malice, and be kind to one another, tenderhearted forgiving one another, as God in Christ has forgiven you.*

> (I Thessalonians 5:19): *Do not quench the*

Spirit.

I do not believe the Spirit will forsake us but I do believe we can grieve the Spirit, we can quench the effectiveness of the Spirit, by being inattentive and unresponsive.

Henri Nouwen wrote this in a book for ministers but its wider application is apparent:

> *What needs to be guarded is the life of the Spirit within us. Especially we who want to witness to the presence of God's Spirit in the world need to tend the fire within with utmost care. It is not so strange that many ministers have become burnt-out-cases, people who say many words and share many experiences, but in whom the fire of God's Spirit has died….Our first and foremost task is faithfully to care for the inward fire so that when it is really needed it can offer warmth and light to lost travelers.*[6]

Your first task is to tend the fire within. Set aside some time each day to keep the inner fire of enthusiasm, the fire of Holy Spirit, burning in your life. If you don't know any other way to do it, read a passage of scripture and then just talk to God, to Jesus, to the Spirit, the way you talk to anyone in ordinary conversation: "Help me today to be listening to the inner promptings of your Spirit. Help me be aware that you are with me, within me, encouraging me, empowering me, strengthening me. Help me to live today as one possessed. As one possessed by your Spirit."

It was in a different context, but I have often thought it would be a good morning ritual for all of us. A woman remembers that as a teenager she was plagued by outbreaks of acne. One day, when she felt unable to leave the house because of anguish over her face, her father led her to the bathroom and asked if he could teach her a new way to wash her face. He leaned over the sink and splashed water over his face, telling her, "On the first splash, say, 'In the name of the Father,' on the second, 'in the name of the Son,' and, on the third, 'in the name of the Holy Spirit.' Then look up into the mirror and remember that you are a child of God, full of grace and beauty." To begin each day on the high note of claiming our heritage, I would only change the last line to: "I am a child of God, full of grace and power."

"The idea is not...that everything in the life of the believer is different. The idea is rather that no dimension of life is closed off to the transforming power of the Spirit..."[7] Spiritually covers all of life. Everything we are and everything we do. It is not something that has to do with our "religious" lives, it has to do with life. That's all we have anyway; we do not live in compartments.

But If Not...

Something More

After having read countless of his books to my two sons, a few years ago I stumbled across Dr. Suess's poem about words, language, and alphabets. It is titled *On Beyond Zebra*:

> Said Conrad Cornelius o'Donald o'Dell,
> My very young friend who is learning to spell:
> "The A is for Ape. And the B is for Bear.
> The C is for Camel. The H is for Hare.
> The M is for Mouse. And the R is for Rat.
>
> I know all the twenty-six letters like that...
> So now I know everything anyone knows
> From beginning to end. From the start to the close.
>
> Because Z is as far as the alphabet goes..."
> Then he almost fell flat on his face on the floor
> When I picked up the chalk and drew one letter more!
>
> A letter he never had dreamed of before!
> And I said, "You can stop, if you want, with the Z
> Because most people stop with the Z.
> But not me!

*In the places I go there are things that I see
That I never could spell if I stopped with Z.
I'm telling you this 'cause you're one of my friends.
My alphabet starts where your alphabet ends!"*[8]

The Christian's spiritual alphabet starts where the world's spiritual alphabet ends. Jesus promised all of his followers the gift of Holy Spirit to indwell and empower. Holy Spirit to translate our groaning into prayers (Romans 8:26). Holy Spirit to lead, guide, counsel, and admonish us. Holy Spirit to bear witness with our spirits that we are children of God and joint-heirs with Christ (Romans 8:16). Holy Spirit who pleads for us in harmony with God's will and purpose for our lives (Romans 8:27). Holy Spirit who is God with us in a way we never could have imagined. This is spirituality with a capital S.

Someone gave a brief list under the heading "Would You Believe?" I added an additional one:

> *Would you believe the Bible says that the same Spirit who worked wonders at Pentecost dwells in you today?*

> *Would you believe the Bible says that you can do all things through Christ who strengthens you? (Philippians 4:13).*

But If Not...

Would you believe the Bible says that to as many as received him to them gave he power, even to become the sons and daughters of God?

Would you believe the Bible says that the resurrection power that raised Lazarus from the dead can be at work in you today?

(My addition): Would you believe that the amazing power at work within you is able to accomplish abundantly farm more than all you can ask or imagine?

Believe all these things. As incredible as they sound, they are all true.

But If Not...

Reflections

Sweeping generalities are usually examples of extreme oversimplifications; in spite of that, I give "general" agreement to this one:

> *As some biblical exegetes have observed, the difference between the Old Testament and the New Testament is fundamentally a difference in the operation of the Spirit. In the Old Testament the Spirit manifests itself in the deeds and utterances of certain religious authorities….In the new aeon that follows Easter morning, however, the Spirit is manifestly conferred on all believers.*[9]

The gift of the Spirit has often been associated with manifestations such as speaking in tongues and frenzied "charismatic" behaviors. Biblically, the "fruit of the Spirit" is both more tame and more relational: *…the fruit of the Spirit is love, joy, peace, patience, kindness, generosity, faithfulness, gentleness, and self-control* (Galatians 5:22-23).

Whatever else one wants to say about demonstrations of the Spirit, these are foundational. For most of us, tongue-speaking and states of ecstasy have not been part of our religious experience. I pass no judgment on those for whom they have been. My only word of caution is that the list in Galatians 5 is far more community building and inclusive; every believer is meant to demonstrate these gifts of the

Spirit. As the Spirit is gift, so is this fruit. Please note that the word "fruit" is singular and not plural.

Parker Palmer introduced me to the Quaker concept of a Clearness Committee which seems to me to provide a concrete and necessary check on our perceived inner promptings of the Spirit. The process involves committing to writing the problem with which one is struggling (including any background material) and inviting four or five colleagues to be a part of the discerning process. According to Parker, the committee meets for two or three uninterrupted hours with each participant permitted only to ask honest and open questions. True to Quaker style, ample periods of silence are a part of the process. Parker writes: "As a member of many clearness committees, I have been privileged to witness a remarkable thing: human beings in dialogue with their inner teachers." This quote including a full explanation of the operation of a clearness committee, will be found in his excellent book *The Courage to Teach*.[10]

This process would serve as the needed corrective to the often heard "God told me" statements that announce a decision or course of action that frequently appears to have bypassed the instructions in I John 4:1: *Beloved, do not believe every spirit, but test the spirits to see whether they are from God*....While I have never used an official clearness committee, I have frequently used close and trusted friends to help me listen more clearly to my inner teacher, the Spirit bearing witness to my spirit. Also, the acid test is always how my hearing of the Spirit checks out with the fruit of the Spirit in Galatians 5. I will never be led to anything that is contrary to God's purpose that I be rooted and grounded in love (Ephesians 3:17).

---

[1] W. Paul Jones, *A Season in the Desert: Making Time Holy*, 13.

[2] Ibid, 155.

[3] J. S. Whale, *Christian Doctrine* (Cambridge, University Press, 17.

[4] Diana Eck, *Encountering God* (Boston, Beacon Press, 1993), 130.

[5] Ibid, 34.

[6] Henri Nouwen, *The Way of the Heart* (New York, Seabury Press, 1981), 54-55.

[7] Kelly Monroe, *Finding God At Harvard* (Grand Rapids, Zondervan, 1996), 155.

[8] Spencer Burke and Barry Taylor, *A Heretic's Guide to Eternity* (San Francisco, Jossey-Bass, 2006), 146-147.

[9] Carl Raschke, *The Next Reformation,* 189.

[10] Parker Palmer, *The Courage To Teach* (San Francisco, Jossey-Bass, 1998), 152.

Chapter 14: Have You Heard Any Good Silence Lately?

MODERN OBSERVATIONS:

"There are some things we shall never know until we are quiet, until we listen to our hearts." - -
Pascal

"So fill me with thy life that I shall feel thy slightest touch, hear thy softest whisper, see thy faintest footprint..."

The essential idea is simple: to lead happy, productive lives in a connected world, we need to master the art of disconnecting.[2]

Perpetually connected equals perpetually zoned out.[3]

Contemplation is an exercise in keeping your heart and mind spaces open long enough for the mind to see other hidden material. It is content with the naked now and waits for futures given by God and grace.4

But If Not...

THE BIBLICAL TEXT: I Kings 19:9b-13a:

> *Then the word of the Lord came to him, saying, "What are you doing here, Elijah?" He answered, "I have been very zealous for the Lord, the God of hosts; for the Israelites have forsaken your covenant, thrown down your altars, and killed your prophets with the sword. I alone am left, and they are seeking my life, to take it away."*
>
> *He said, "Go out and stand on the mountain before the Lord, for the Lord himself is about to pass by." Now there was a great wind, so strong that it was splitting mountains and breaking rocks in pieces before the Lord, but the Lord was not in the earthquake; and after the earthquake a fire, but the Lord was not in the fire; and after the fire a sound of sheer silence. When Elijah heard it, he wrapped his face in his mantle and went out and stood at the entrance of the cave.*

God's Question

When God asks the question, I don't think he is seeking information; it is Elijah who needs to hear the question and contemplate an answer. God's question is, "What in the world are you doing here, Elijah?" This is a rebuke as well as a question. God's prophet is hiding in a cave on Mount Horeb, the mountain on which Moses got fire and thunder, God's presence, and the Ten Commandments.

Elijah pours out his tale of woe: "Well, Lord, I've been just about the best prophet you've ever had. I have brought the message your people needed to hear, warned them about the worship of idols, called them to be faithful – but they wouldn't listen. The truth is, I'm the only faithful one left and Jezebel is after me; if her soldiers find me, she has instructed them to kill me. Why do you think I'm here? I'm scared to death!"

I once thought Elijah was a pitiful prophet at this juncture in his career. If God had done for me what he had done for Elijah, I certainly would have been fearless and faithful. That only revealed my naivety and foolishness. I was convinced that the Mount Carmel experience described in I Kings 18 would have lasted me a lifetime and it hardly lasted Elijah overnight.

Just before we meet Elijah hiding in a cave, we meet him on Mount Carmel in the famous contest with the prophets of Baal. Each side is to prepare an altar and a sacrifice; the god who answers by fire will prove himself the true God of Israel. The prophets of Baal have the first go and simply can't get their god to display even a sparkler. When Elijah gets his turn, he prays, and such fire falls from heaven that it consumes the offering, the wood and stone of the altar, as well as the water in the trench. The people respond by falling on their faces and repeating, "The Lord indeed is God."

This demonstration equals at least ten burning bushes. Who could ever again doubt God's power? Elijah, that's who! As soon as Queen Jezebel sends her troops after him, Elijah forgets all about God's magic show on Mount Carmel. When God confronts Elijah on Mount Horeb, he has a greater message than the one he gave on Mount Carmel. It is a message we all need to hear; this biblical story needs to become our story. I give you the message in the form of a question: Have you heard any good silence lately?

What Do We Expect?

Elijah's answer to God's, "What are you doing here?" might have been, "I'm waiting for more fireworks." In the book *Children's Letters to God*, at least two of the letters address this issue: Jennifer: "Dear God, in Bible times did they really talk so fancy?" Joanne: "Dear God, I would like to know why all the things you said are in red?"[5] The answer? In the biblical time of Elijah there was a lot of fancy talk and when God talked he was definitely expected to speak in red. Perhaps this is why we are so taken aback by what God does for Elijah.

God instructs him to stand on the mountain as the usual manifestations of his presence are paraded before Elijah. The fireworks show of the usual ways people expected God to make himself known occurs with little subtleness. With each demonstration, we note, not God's presence, but God's absence. Earthquake, wind, and fire come in quick succession. It is Mount Carmel all over again, except God is not found in any of his expected garb. Is God asking Elijah, "Just because there were no fireworks, did you think I was not with you? Did you believe I had abandoned you? Did you hide in a cave because the spectacular display of my presence was at an end?"

These are good questions for all of us. We confess that at times we are not unlike those who kept asking Jesus, "Show us a sign." We would give anything for special or spectacular phenomenon to assure us God has not departed. Elijah's response to God's, "Why are you here?" can all too easily be our response: "We are afraid and in hiding from life, Lord, because we've got to have a faith we can feel and see. Give us some display of your presence and we'll be set for at least another thirty days."

Elijah needed what we all need: the ability to recognize God's presence apart from the fireworks. The key word in our text has to do with listening. *The Lord was not in the wind, the earthquake, or the fire – but (after) the fire there was the sound of sheer silence. When Elijah HEARD it*…. My question has always been: Just how hard do you have to be listening to hear the sound of sheer silence? The chances of hearing the sound of sheer silence at the present moment in our culture are practically nil. I am encouraged by how much is being written about noise pollution and the need for silence.

A November 2, 2009, *Newsweek* article by Julia Baird is titled "The Devil Loves Cell Phones"; the subtitle is: "Silence isn't just golden – it's heavenly." The article contains several quotes from a book I haven't read, *A Book of Silence* by Sara Maitland. She believes the mobile phone is a "major breakthrough for the powers of hell"! Also: "I am convinced that as a whole society we are losing something precious in our increasingly silence-avoiding culture and that somehow whatever this silence might be, it needs holding, nourishing, and unpacking." Here is the conclusion of the article by Julia Baird:

> *I know it sounds like the lament of a Luddite. (Mine: a Luddite is basically one who is opposed to technological change.) But if generations of mystics and seekers have insisted that there's something that connects silence with the sublime, you have to wonder what we are distracting ourselves from – and who we could be if, every now and then we paused.*

Trying Silence

In September, 2009, I attended a Mercer University Preaching Consultation. At that conference, Kyle Matthews told about a friend of his who went on a three day silent retreat at the Abbey of Gethsemani in Kentucky where Thomas Merton lived and is buried. His friend is a sound engineer. When he returned and Kyle asked him how it was, he said, "Dude, after two days of total silence, you start to hear things!"

Marva Dawn said the same thing in a conference in Macon, Georgia. She is quoted: "We don't know how to do silence very well as God's people." She called silence a "rare gift" and noted that God will often say things to us in silence that we haven't wanted to (or been able to) hear amid the noise.[6]

USA Today conducted a survey in 1998 (but still up to date) in which people were asked to name the ten things they feared the most. The most feared was death, and then flying. After flying – silence. (Followed closely by public speaking, dogs, snakes, and spiders).[7]

Many churches have problems with silence; most of it relates to being "seeker friendly" or having "cultural relevance." A major power house of "relevance" suggests that the way you evaluate your worship service is to record it, then play it back side-by-side with the TV tuned to MTV. The more similarity there is, the more likely that the service will communicate the Gospel to people, especially those under 40. They also recommend that churches eliminate any period of silence during worship that lasts longer than five seconds! I would note the source of this information but it so upset me that I tossed the book! But I assure you this was the advice.

A source I have retained gives advice under the heading "Sensible Worship."

> *Postmoderns literally "feel" their way through life. Want to create change? Give postmoderns a new experience they haven't had before....Total Experience is the new watchword in postmodern worship. New World preachers don't "write sermons." They create total experiences....It will not be easy for Protestantism to make this transition to worship that meets the "wow" standard.*[8]

In the margin of the book next to that last sentence I wrote, "Should they?" I would like to be able to discuss with postmoderns (wherever and whoever they are), just how much of MTV and "Wow" they really want in worship. Do they want this to be their only and their total worship experience? What do they want when family members die, they lose their jobs, they get divorced, a new war breaks out, the financial markets crumble, we are attacked anew by terrorists, and the world falls apart? I am not a Luddite but my great fear is that (permit the cliché), if we are not careful, we will throw out the baby with the bath water – we will toss the relevancy of the gospel and worship out in our attempt to be relevant.

Next to the call for MTV and Wow I would place this biblical command: *Be still and know that I am God* (Psalm 46).

Britain's Royal Navy has a practice known as the "all-still." When something goes wrong on a ship, particularly on a submarine, the captain announces an all-still. For three minutes no one is allowed to move or speak. The writer supplying this information then comments: "Three minutes of silence and stillness can have an exponential effect in the middle of a turbulent situation."[9] I place that beside this comment about the power of silence among Quakers: "Words (spoken) 'out of silence' take on significance *because* of the silence, because they have been weighed."[10]

Not earthquake, wind, or fire could give Elijah what he so desperately needed that day on the mountain. First of all, he needed to face himself. He needed to face his self-pity ("I'm the only faithful one left!"), his arrogance, his lack of trust in God, and his fear of Jezebel. He needed to know why he was hiding in a cave. We all need silence because silence introduces us to ourselves. It allows us – causes us – to face ourselves. It allows us to hear things we can't hear in the noise. It forces us to hear things we don't want to hear. This is all to the good!

In the front lobby of the guest house of the Abbey of

Gethsemani is a guest register that has a column for "Observations." Under the heading are the most eloquent arguments for the benediction of silence:

> *"A return to the deep well of peace."*
> *"I came to talk, discuss and argue. I learned to listen."*
> *"For once I let God do all the talking."*
> *"A welcome comma in my life."*
> *"Beyond words."*
> *"A point of stillness in the search for the stillpoint."*
> *"Ahhhh."* [11]

Our challenge remains the same as it was for Elijah: to learn how to listen above and beyond the noise of the world in order to be able to hear the sound of sheer silence. When we do, I believe we will know what Elijah so desperately needed to know that day on the mountain and we all so desperately need to know in our day. It's all summarized in Psalm 46:

> *Be still, and know that I am God.*
> *I am exalted among the nations.*
> *I am exalted in the earth.*
> *The Lord of hosts is with us.*
> *The God of Jacob is our refuge.*

But If Not...

Reflections

In sharp contrast to the suggestions for church growth that I cited in this chapter, is this: "Some recent 'trend scholarship' suggests that a strong yearning among so-called postmoderns is for spirituality that values ritual, quiet, perhaps even mystical experience."[12] William Powers' *Hamlet's Blackberry* is just one of the many responses to an information overload and over-connected world. A seven-page *Newsweek* article in the March 7, 2011, issue is titled "I Can't Think!" The opening gamut is: "The Twitterization of our culture has revolutionized our lives, but with an unintended consequence – our overloaded brains freeze when we have to make decisions." The last line in the article is: "If you think you're a maximizer, the best prescription for you might be the 'off' switch on your smart phone."

This may be exactly the right time to reintroduce the ancient Elijah story and ask the question that appears all too relevant: "Have you heard any good silence lately?"

---

[1]Bob Benson, *Laughter in the Walls* (Mexico, Gaither Family Resources, 1996), 39.
[2]William Powers, *Hamlet's Blackberry* (New York, HarperCollins, 2010), 6.
[3]Ibid, 68.
[4]Richard Rohr, *The Naked Now,* 34.
[5]David Heller, *Dear God: Children's Letters to God* (New York, A Perigee Book, 1994).
[6]*Baptists Today,* November 2009, 30.
[7]Matthew Kelly, *The Rhythm of Life* (New York, Fireside,

2004), 191.
[8]Leonard Sweet, *Postmodern Pilgrims,* 43-44.
[9]Matthew Kelly, *the Rhythm of Life,* 203.
[10]Brian Kaylor, *For God's Sake, Shut Up!* (Macon, Smyth & Helwys, 2007), 14.
[11]Gregg Levoy, *Callings,* 30.
[12]Bob Sitz, *Not Trying Too Hard,* 14.

Chapter 15: Who's Holding the Cue Cards?

MODERN OBSERVATIONS:

> At most Christian weddings, the chief ritual specialist is not the pastor or priest, but the wedding planner, followed closely by the photographer, the florist, and the caterer. More wedding theology is supplied in fact by Bride magazine or GQ than by an dozen academic treatises on holy matrimony.[1]

> "I was street smart – unfortunately the street was Rodeo Drive." Carrie Fisher.

> Jesus never worshiped at the altar of human approval. But we sure do.[2]

> In choosing approval rather than authenticity – our center of gravity is in "them" and not in ourselves. And what has been lost? Just the one true and vital part of us: our own yes-feeling which is our capacity for growth.[3]

But If Not...

THE BIBLICAL TEXTS: Luke 7:31-35; Matthew 5:43-45; *New Living Translation:*

> *"How shall I describe this generation?" Jesus asked, "With what shall I compare them? They are like a group of children playing a game in the public square. They complain to their friends, 'We played wedding songs, and you weren't happy, so we played funeral songs, but you weren't sad.' For John the Baptist didn't drink wine and he often fasted, and you say, 'He's demon possessed.' And I, the Son of Man feast and drink, and you say, 'He's a glutton and a drunkard, and a friend of the worst sort of sinners!' But wisdom is shown to be right by the lives of those who follow it."*
>
> *"You have heard that the law of Moses says, 'Love your neighbor and hate your enemy.' But I say to you, love your enemies! Pray for those who persecute you! In that way, you will be acting as true children of your Father in heaven. For he gives his sunlight to both the evil and the good, and he sends rain on the just and the unjust, too."*

Quick and Easy Responses

A minister friend sent me a cartoon depicting a church service. In the first frame, a man is receiving a cell phone call. In frame two he answers and whispers, "Hey! I'm listening to the church announcements." In frame three, he says, "Call me back during the sermon."

This immediately brought to mind a still vivid experience in my first church out of seminary. A fire chief was a member of my congregation; each Sunday he sat on the second row to my left and listened for fire calls all during the service. He also read the worship folder and announcement sheet during the sermon. It became a major distraction. One Sunday, with my frustration at a new level, I said rather pointedly, "It's a shame some people don't come to church to worship." The fire chief was reading through the bulletin for the third time and he never flinched. Later, I thought about how many services he had ruined. Almost instantly, something within forced me to rethink that to how many worship services I had ruined. He held the worship folder – the cue card – and I reacted right on cue!

Or, in the context of Luke 7, he played funeral and I wept! It is so easy to let others determine how we feel and what we will do. It's almost automatic to respond to the cue cards others are holding. In our text from Matthew, Jesus warns about living in reaction to others. If I have an enemy, it is natural to see the cue card, "Hate me!" "Get angry!" "Get upset!" "Get even!" The major reason I should not hate my enemy is not for what it might do to my enemy but for what it will do to me. Many stay bent out of shape due to resentment, hurt, and anger over past grievances; they remain in the reaction mode.

Who's In Charge of My Life?

The real problem in all this is that others are in charge of my life. When I reacted to the fire chief on the second row, I completely forgot all the other people gathered there who were not listening for fire calls or reading their bulletins. I forgot why I was there and what I was supposed to be about. I lost my focus. I lost my purpose. I lost my effectiveness. My greatest loss of all was that I surrendered the right to determine my own conduct.

Our texts remind us that Jesus knew who he was. He knew what he was about. That determined what he would do and how he would respond. He didn't play to the crowd; he lived out his life on the basis of what he was certain to be his call and his mission. He did not allow anyone or anything to throw him off course. He was always true to himself as the unique son of his heavenly Father.

Staying in charge of our lives takes wit and wisdom and, ironically, genuine humility. From the life of George Washington Carver, the famous African-American who developed over three hundred products from the peanut, comes one of my favorite stories. He had a speaking engagement in a southern city and his train was late. When he finally disembarked from the train, he quickly found a taxi and jumped in. He asked to be driven to the civic auditorium. The driver looked at this black man and said, "I can't drive you to the auditorium." Carver thought for a moment and said, "Well, change places with me and I'll drive you to the auditorium!" He did! And arrived at his speaking engagement on time – which was his goal. Tough to do! Sure! Isn't it always tough to stay in charge of our lives and stay on course with who we believe we are and what we believe we have been called to do?

The Freedom Not To Respond

The greatest freedom I know, and the freedom that will truly set you free, is the freedom not to have to respond to the cue cards of others. As long as we are responding to their cue cards, we are captive, we are slaves. The moment we know that regardless of what others do or say, we can still choose, we are free – even in the most unlikely places and circumstances.

In his well-known book, *Man's Search for Meaning*, Victor Frankl writes about his experiences in the death camp at Auschwitz.[4] He remembers men who walked through the huts, comforting others, and giving away their last piece of bread. They were captives – and yet they were free. The greatest freedom is to choose one's own attitude, one's own way, in any given set of circumstances. We don't have to react. We are free to respond appropriately.

But If Not...

Both popular and religious books carry this idea:

Be present as the watcher of your mind – of your thoughts and emotions as well as your reactions in various situations. Be at least as interested in your reactions as in the situation or person that causes you to react.[5]

If I am not present as the watcher of my mind, my thoughts, my emotions, and my reactions, I can get in a whole lot of trouble.

Two men are out driving and run into each other. The first climbs out of the wreckage of his car and helps the second man, who is badly shaken, to the side of the road. "You had a nasty shock," he says, and offers a hip flask to the other man, who takes a long, grateful gulp. "Go on, have another." "But what about you?" asks the second man. "Don't you drink?" "No," replies the owner of the hip flask. "Not until after the police arrive."[6]

I don't want to believe that all the people who try to push our buttons are as deceptive as the man in that story but they are usually not focused on our well-being. They are more concerned with themselves than they are with us.

But If Not...

Jesus reminds us that God sends rain on the just and the unjust; his actions are not determined by those who deserve and those who don't. God's love is unconditional. The message of the cross is: "There's nothing you can do to stop me from loving you." I believe Jesus instructs us to love our enemies and do good because he doesn't want them to change us. Nothing his creation does changes the nature and purposes of God. Jesus says that the way his disciples live should always reflect who they are and what they are about – and not what is happening to them at the moment.

If I wake up each day with the questions: "Wonder what kind of a person I'll be today? Wonder what kind of reactions will color my life?" – then I will be captive to whatever and whoever comes my way. That is why it is so necessary each and every day to get ourselves ready for the day. Bible study, devotional reading, prayer, and meditation are a must. Because we don't know what we're going to have to confront each day, we must do our best to get centered and focused on who we are and what we are supposed to be about.

We can't suddenly call up resources we haven't put into our lives. It is easy to tell when people have such resources and when they don't. The Duke of Wellington was known for his ability to remain calm under pressure, even at the risk of his life. (He was the one who defeated Napoleon at Waterloo). The story is told that one day an inmate who had escaped from a nearby asylum broke into his office

But If Not...

announcing that he must kill the general. Wellington looked up from his papers and inquired, "Does it have to be today?" When the would-be assassin hesitated, Wellington added, "A little later on, then. I'm busy at the moment." The man left, was arrested, and Wellington got back to work.

You don't create a center of calm for that at the last minute! Spend some time at the beginning of each day (if only ten minutes!) getting ready for whatever or whoever might come your way during the hours that follow.

The Internal Prompter

For those of us in the community of faith, we have the necessary resource. We have an internal prompter – the Holy Spirit. The Spirit bears witness with our spirit, counsels us, guides us, helps us. Helps us to be inner-directed rather than outer-directed. An excellent summary of what we are talking about comes from this paraphrase of Matthew 5:43-48 in Eugene Peterson's *The Message:*

> *Jesus says, "You're familiar with the old written law, 'Love your friend,' and its unwritten companion, 'Hate your enemy.' I'm challenging that. I'm telling you to love your enemies. Let them bring out the best in you, not the worst. When someone gives you a hard time, respond with the energies of prayer, for then you are working out of your*

But If Not...

true selves, your God-created selves. This is what God does. He gives his best – the sun to warm and the rain to nourish – everyone, regardless: the good and bad, the nice and nasty. If all you do is love the lovable, do you expect a bonus? Anybody can do that. If you simply say hello to those who greet you, do you expect a medal? Any run-of-the-mill sinner does that.

"In a word, what I'm saying is, Grow up. You're kingdom subjects. Now live like it. Live out your God-created identity. Live generously and graciously toward others, the way God lives toward you."

But If Not...

Reflections

This chapter ends on the Kingdom note because it's our major cue card. It is the answer to the question posed by the title "Who's Holding the Cue Cards?" Paul Jones in *Making Time Holy* contends: "The three Ps of the American dream – possessions, prestige, and power – are not really rewards at all, but temptations to soul-selling."[7] Yet these three Ps are usually the standards by which we judge success. That is why they are so powerful, so seductive. The Sermon on the Mount continues to be the call for different criteria for success. When anyone tells me that the Sermon the Mount turns the world upside down, my response is, "No, it turns the world right side up!" It describes God's intention for the way we are to live with each other. The way we are to live out our faith.

Living as a Kingdom citizen in a world where the Kingdom has not yet fully been realized is far from easy. Temptations abound to be less than we are called to be – even in the most unlikely places. Barbara Brown Taylor relates that when she was at Yale Divinity School in the 1970s, the books she wanted were never in the library, nor was there any record at the front desk that they had been checked out. When she asked the librarian about this, he told her that the Divinity School had the highest theft rate of any graduate school in the university.[8]

The librarian offered his take as to the reason, but I'm not certain there is any reason except that the temptation to turn in on ourselves and momentarily forget our calling in relation to others is ever present. No doubt, many of the books were taken, hopefully, with the intention of returning them later. My experience as a seminary student with required reading from "books on reserve," was that you were lucky if you could locate them. The cue cards of achievement, performance, "if I don't take it someone else will" – quickly surface to misdirect us.

Remaining true to ourselves, to our best selves, to our God created and intended selves, requires many things. One of these is paying attention to the source of the promptings to which we respond.

---

[1] Mark Jordan, *Telling Truths in Church* (Boston, Beacon Press, 2004), 36.
[2] Paul Coughlin, *No More Christian Nice Guy* (Minneapolis, Bethany House, 2005), 183.
[3] Gregg Levoy, *Callings*, 195.
[4] Viktor Frankl, *Man's Search for Meaning* (Boston, Beacon Press, 1959).
[5] Eckhart Tolle, *The Power of Now* (Novato, CA., New World Library, 2004), 55.
[6] Jimmy Carr and Lucy Greeves, *Only Joking* (New York, Gotham Books, 2006), 197.
[7] W. Paul Jones, *A Season in the Desert: Making Time Holy*, 7.
[8] Barbara Brown Taylor, *Speaking of Sin*, 52.

But If Not...

Part V: On Being Inner-Directed
Points to Ponder

There seems to be an unspoken assumption that the really great parts of the Bible are for super saints.

Holes in the ceiling of churches in tenth century Rome were not an indication of needed roof repairs.

Our first task is to tend the fire within.

The Christian's spiritual alphabet starts where the world's spiritual alphabet ends.

Elijah needed what we all need: the ability to recognize God's presence apart from the fireworks.

As God's people, we don't know how to do silence very well.

Words spoken "out of silence" take on significance because of the silence, because they are weighed.

Have YOU heard any good silence lately?

We experience many losses when others hold the cue cards; the greatest loss is the right to determine our own conduct.

But If Not...

The greatest freedom I know is the freedom not to have to respond to the cue cards of others.

We can't suddenly call up resources we haven't put into our lives.

Remaining true to ourselves, to our best selves, to our God-created and intended selves, requires many things. One of these is paying attention to the source of the promptings to which we respond.

Conclusion: The Real Secret
(Psalm 37:1-6, 34)

Do not fret because of the wicked;
  do not be envious of wrongdoers,
for they will soon fade like the grass,
  and wither like the green herb.
Trust in the Lord, and do good;
  so you will live in the land, and enjoy security.
Take delight in the Lord,
  and he will give you the desires of your heart.
Commit your way to the Lord;
  trust in him, and he will act.
He will make your vindication shine like the light,
  and the justice of your cause like the noonday.
Wait for the Lord, and keep to his way,
  and he will exalt you to inherit the land;
  you will look on the destruction of the wicked.

Cultural Prescriptions

I kept seeing the question on T-shirts and couldn't imagine how I could have missed such a seemingly national event. Finally, I got the courage to ask someone in a private moment the question that would not go away. The question? "Who shot JR?" It was quite a relief to discover it was simply a prime-time soap opera but disturbing to discover I had been unaware of such a cultural phenomenon. I didn't want this to happen again.

So with all the talk, stacks of the books at Sam's and Costco (not to mention Oprah's endorsement), I knew it was time to read *The Secret*. The good news is that you only have to get to page four to discover the secret:

> *The Secret is the law of attraction! Everything that's coming into your life you are attracting by your life. And it's attracted to you by virtue of the images you're holding in your mind. It's what you're thinking.*[1]

Not a totally bad idea, although it seemed to me to be a new twist on the old idea of the power of positive thinking. (A little research reveals the law of attraction has been no secret!) There is no question about the value of a positive, hopeful attitude about life and the negative effects of a doom and gloom mindset. On page 72 of the book I was informed that every time I looked in my mail box expecting to see a bill, it would be there. I was told that, using the law of attraction, I was to do myself a favor and expect a check. Great idea! That's exactly what I did. But, alas, I regret to report that the next day, as regular as clockwork, I didn't get a check from Louisville Gas and Electric Company, I got another bill!

Although I have stretched this to the point of absurdity, we all admit there is value in expecting the good instead of the bad. When you read a book like *The Secret* one of the questions to ask is: "This is true but what else is also true?" Two quotes that immediately come to mind: Eugene Peterson: "Most lies are ninety percent the truth"; Oliver Wendell Holmes: "I don't give a fig for the simplicity this side of complexity, but I would die for the simplicity on the other side of complexity."

A major problem with *The Secret* (and most of the "this is all you have to do" books) is that it ignores the complexities of paradox, ambiguity, unfairness, sin, evil, unpredictability, and just outright randomness that unfortunately are all a part of life. And you don't have to attract these complexities to find them camping outside your door. My contention is that the real secret for living can be found in a book that is fully aware of the complexities of existence.

A Candid Assessment

In Psalm 37, it is obvious we're talking about the real world because the writer begins his reflection with a candid assessment of what is going on: *Do not fret because of the*

But If Not...

wicked; do not be envious of wrongdoers." The psalm begins with the admission that often the wicked of this world do exceedingly well. The prosperity of the wicked is one of the constant complaints in the Psalms and in the Bible as a whole (see Jeremiah 12:1). Both verbs translated as *fret* and *envious* have the similar root meaning of "being heated." Literally, we are being told, "Don't get all hot and bothered." We are reminded that the first great secret in life is not to spend time wringing our hands over all that is wrong in life but rather we are to *trust in the Lord and do good.*

We begin by trusting in the one who assures us that goodness does *ultimately* pay off. If, as instructed, we are able to w*ait for the Lord, and keep to his way*, we are demonstrating our confidence (trust) in God and our ability to take the long view. I once read the account of a woman who went to a counselor complaining about her husband and his refusal to change. The counselor advised that she stop nagging him and see what the results would be. So she stopped nagging. On the next visit she was asked, "How is it going?" "I give up. It doesn't work. I've been nice to my husband a whole two weeks and he hasn't changed a bit."

Most of us want to put the coin of goodness in the vending machine of life, pull a lever, and receive an immediate payoff. I have often used this quote: "To Jesus the judgments of God are sure, but he would not have his disciples expect to see the books balanced every weekend" (Ralph Sockman). Or in two weeks! Surely a great secret in

But If Not...

life is trusting God enough to make long term investments.

In a *Peanuts* cartoon, Lucy is kneeling in her garden with Charlie Brown looking on. She says, "Boy, I'm gonna fool the birds this time." She stands and stamps her foot hard on the ground. "They won't get these flower seeds. I've really got those stupid birds licked this time." Then she leans over and whispers in Charlie Brown's ear: "I left the seeds in the package."

I weep for those who have adopted Lucy's strategy. They have left the seeds in the package because they fear there is too much risk in planting the seeds of goodness. Their lament: "What's the use? The birds of prey are everywhere." The psalmist's words of wisdom provide the opposite approach: "Take the risk of doing good in a world that is full of so much wrong. Trust in God and wait for him to give you a bumper crop of what you have sown."

You may be asking: "Do you mean right now? In my present circumstances? I don't see the possibilities right now; a few things have got to change before I can *trust in the Lord and do good.*"

> *The story is told of a golf course in India. Apparently, once the English had colonized the country and established their businesses, they yearned for recreation and decided to build a golf course in Calcutta. Golf in Calcutta presented a unique obstacle. Monkeys would drop out of the trees, scurry*

across the course, and seize the golf balls. The monkeys would play with the balls, tossing them here and there.

At first, the golfers tried to control the monkeys. Their first strategy was to build high fences around the fairways, and the greens. This approach, which seemed initially to hold much promise, was abandoned when the golfers discovered that a fence is no challenge to an ambitious monkey. Next, the golfers tried luring the monkeys away from the course. But the monkeys found nothing as amusing as watching humans go wild whenever the little white balls were disturbed. In desperation, the British began trapping the monkeys. But for every monkey they carted off, another would appear. Finally, the golfers gave in to reality and developed a rather novel ground rule: Play the ball where the monkey drops it.[2]

A good rule for golf in Calcutta is a good rule for the game of life. Good breaks, bad breaks, good luck, bad luck, fair, unfair – whatever – live right now, where you are, just as things are. Live on the basis of what is and not on the basis of what is not. Make the best of less than ideal circumstances. What other kind of circumstances are there?

But If Not...

In other words, play the ball where the monkey drops it.

In an imperfect, flawed world, don't major on fretting; major on trusting in the Lord and doing good. In Bible studies, I often ask someone to tell me Jesus' most repeated command. After several incorrect answers, someone usually gets it right. Jesus' most repeated command to his disciples is, "Fear not." To repeat what I have written elsewhere: There are 365 "Fear nots" – one for every day in the year. A great secret of life is to begin each day with the motto: "Today I will not live in fear and anxiety; I will trust in the Lord and do good."

However, this is not the real secret tucked away in this psalm. The real secret is found in verse five: *Commit your way to the Lord; trust in him and he will act.* The word translate *commit* means *roll*. A possible translation is: *roll you way of life upon the Lord in utter abandon.* Do what you know you can do and ought to do and, then, LET IT GO! In the ancient Chinese Book of the Way (the *Tao Te Ching* – after the Bible, the most widely translated book in the world), we find this piece of wisdom:

> *Fill your bowl to the brim*
> *and it will spill.*
> *Keep sharpening your knife*
> *and it will blunt.*
> *Chase after money and security*
> *and your heart will never unclench.*

But If Not...

*Care about people's approval
and you will be their prisoner.
Do your work, then step back.
The only path to serenity.*³

Perhaps the reason this concept is the *real* secret and not widely practiced is because it is so difficult. Yet, it is the most common sense approach of all. After you have done what you can do and feel you ought to do (always done imperfectly), what else is there to do but step back? For the believer, this means to step back and trust God with the results. *The New Jerusalem Bible* translates Psalm 37:5: *Commit your destiny to Yahweh, be confident in him and he will act, making your uprightness clear as daylight, and the justice of your cause as the noon.*

To be able to do this, we have to believe Romans 8:28: *...in everything, as we know, (God) cooperates for good with those who love (him) and are called according to his purpose* (*Revised English Bible*). Most people cannot/do not do what they can do and then step back, let it go. Most are like the auto mechanic in a story someone sent me. Just so you know this is a factual first-person account, it happened at a Chevrolet dealership in Canton, Mississippi. Here is the verbatim account:

> "When my husband and I arrived at an automobile dealership to pick up our car, we

But If Not...

were told the keys had been locked in it. We went to the service department and found a mechanic working feverishly to unlock the driver's side door. As I watched from the passenger side, I instinctively tried the door handle and discovered that it was unlocked. 'Hey,' I announced to the technician, 'it's open!' His reply, 'I know – I already got that side.'"

The so-obvious moral: don't continue to sweat it out after you've done what you ought to do – after you've done all that is necessary! In order to do this, we have to be willing to give up control of the future – which we don't have anyway! Real faith, real trust in God, means we do leave the future to him – where it belongs anyway. That, of course, is the real message of the book of Revelation. The acquired plus of letting go of outcomes and results is that it frees you to live powerfully in the present. You can live fully and joyfully in the present moment because you aren't wasting emotional and spiritual energy on the future.

Somewhere I stumbled across this meditation on the divine name that was revealed to Moses at the burning bush:

> *I was regretting the past*
> *and fearing the future.*
> *Suddenly my Lord was speaking:*
> *"My name is I AM." He paused.*

I waited. He continued.
"When you live in the past,
with it's mistakes and regrets,
it is hard. I am not there.
My name is not I Was.
When you live in the future,
with it's problems and fears,
it is hard. I am not there.
My name is not I Will Be.
When you live in this moment,
it is not hard. I am here.
My name is I Am." (Helen Mallicoat)

Psalm 37 is the call to present-tense living: *Do not fret because of the wicked; trust in the Lord and do good; commit your way to the Lord; wait for the Lord and keep to his way.*

The real secret is that there is no single secret to life. The real truth is that there is no single truth that excludes all other truths. There are many secrets we discover as we continue to search and there are many truths that reveal themselves as we continue to ask questions. There are many words of wisdom that can give to life a frame of reference that helps us as we continue our searching and our questioning. For those of us in the community of faith, we believe that a basic source of that wisdom is to be found in the writings of Scripture. I can think of no greater wisdom for our time than the simple and profound admonitions of Psalm 37: *Trust in the Lord, and do good; Commit your way*

But If Not...

to the Lord; Wait for the Lord, and keep to his way.

My prayer is that Psalm 37 may be one of the real secrets of your life.

Amen and Amen.

---

[1] Rhonda Byrne, *The Secret* (New York, Atria Books, 2006), 4.
[2] Gregory Knox Jones, *Play the Ball Where the Monkey Drops It* (New York, HarperSanFrancisco, 2001), 3.
[3] Joan Chittister, *The Rule of Benedict* (New York, Crossroad, 1992), 36.

Bibliography of Quoted Sources

Anglican Digest, The. Eureka Springs, AR.
Baptists Today. Macon, GA.
Beck, Edward. *God Underneath.* New York: Image Books, 2002.
Benson, Bob. *Laughter in the Walls.* Mexico: Gaither Family Resources, 1996.
Bill, Brent. *Imagination & Spirit.* Richmond, IN.: Friends United Press, 2002.
Blake, Chris. *Searching for a God to Love.* Nampa, ID.: Pacific Press, 2000.
Broadman Bible Commentary, The. Nashville: Broadman Press, 1969.
Brueggemann, Walter. *An Unsettling God.* Minneapolis: Fortress Press, 2009.
_____. *Mandate to Difference.* Louisville: Westminster John Knox, 2007.
Bruno, Thomas. *Jesus, Ph.D. Psychologist.* Alachua, FL.: Bridge-Logos Publishers, 2000.
Buechner, Frederick. *Secrets in the Dark.* (New York: HarperOne, 2006.
Burke, Spencer and Taylor, Barry. *A Heretic's Guide to Eternity.* San Francisco: Jossey-Bass, 2006.
Byrne, Rhonda. *The Secret.* New York: Atria Books, 2006.
Capps, Donald. *A Time To Laugh.* New York: Continnum, 2005.
Carey, George. *I Believe.* Seattle: Morehouse Publishing, 1991.
Carr, Jimmy and Greeves, Lucy. *Only Joking.* New York: Gotham Books, 2006.
Chittister, Joan. *In Search of Belief.* Liguori, MO.:

Liguori/Triumph, 1999.

_____. *Listen With the Heart.* Lanham: Speed & Ward, 2003.

_____. *The Rule of Benedict.* New York: Crossroad, 1992.

Claiborne, Shane. *The Irresistible Revolution.* Grand Rapids: Zondervan, 2006.

Collier, Robert. *The Secret of the Ages.* New York: Jeremy Tarcher Publisher, 2007.

Coughlin, Paul. *No More Christian Nice Guy.* Minneapolis: Bethany House, 2005.

Covey, Stephen. *The Speed of Trust.* New York: Free Press, 2006.

Cox, James ed. *Best Sermons 4.* New York: HarperCollins, 1991.

Craddock, Fred. *Reflections on My Call to Preach.* St. Louis: Chalice Press, 2009.

De Caussade, Jean-Pierre. *The Sacrament of the Present Moment.* San Francisco: Harper & Row, 1982.

Eck, Diana. *Encountering God.* Boston: Beacon Press, 1993.

Frey, William. *The Dance of Hope.* Colorado Springs: Waterbrook Press, 2003.

Frank, Thomas Edward. *The Soul of the Congregation.* Nashville: Abingdon Press, 2000.

Frankl, Viktor. *Man's Search for Meaning.* Boston: Beacon Press, 1959.

Godsey, Kirby. *Centering Our Souls.* Macon: Mercer University Press, 2005.

Gomes, Peter. *The Scandalous Gospel of Jesus.* New York: HarperOne, 2007.

Gordon, Arthur. *A Touch of Wonder.* Carmel: Guideposts Associates, 1974.

Greeley, Andrew. *Confessions of a Parish Priest.* New York: Simon and Schuster, 1986.

_____. *Jesus: A Meditation on his Stories and his Relationships with Women.* New York: Tom Doherty Associates, 2007.

Hall, Douglas. *Thinking the Faith.* Minneapolis: Augsburg, 1989.

Heller, David. *Children's Letters to God.* New York: A Perigee Book, 1994.

Heller, Thomas. *Just Build the Ark and The Animals Will Come.* New York: Villard Books, 1994.

Henry, Patrick. *Benedict's Dharma.* New York: Riverhead Books, 2001.

Interpreter's Bible, The. Nashville: Abingdon Press, 1952.

Jones, Gregory Knox. *Play the Ball Where the Monkey Drops It.* New York: HarperSanFrancisco, 2001.

Jones, W. Paul. *A Season in the Desert: Making Time Holy.* Brewster: Paraclete Press, 2000.

_____. *Trumpet at Full Moon.* Louisville: John Knox, 1992.

Jordan, Mark. *Telling Truths in Church.* Boston: Beacon Press, 2004.

Kaylor, Brian. *For God's Sake, Shut Up!* Macon: Smyth & Helwys, 2007.

Kelly, Matthew. *The Rhythm of Life.* New York: Fireside, 2004.

Kendall, R. T. and Rosen, David. *The Christian and the Pharisee.* New York: Faith Words, 2006.

Kimball, Don. *Power and Presence: A Theology of Relationships.* New York: HarperCollins, 1987.

Kurtz, Ernest. *The Spirituality of Imperfection.* New York: Bantam Books, 1994.

Lamott, Anne. *Grace Eventually*. New York: Riverhead Books, 2007.
_____. *Plan B*. New York: Riverhead Books, 2005.
Lederer, Richard. *The Miracle of Language*. New York: Pocket Books, 1991.
Levoy, Gregg. *Callings*. New York: Three Rivers Press, 1997.

Lewis, C.S. *The Inspirational Writings of C. S. Lewis*. New York: Inspiration Press, 1987.
Linn, Jan G. *Big Christianity*. Louisville: Westminster John Knox, 2006.
MacDonald Gordon. *Restoring Joy*. Nashville: Thomas Nelson, 2005.
Manning, Brennan. *The Ragamuffin Gospel*. Sisters, OR.: Multnomah Publishers, 2000.
McCullough, Donald. *The Trivialization of God*. Colorado Springs, Navpress, 1995.
McLaren, Brian. *Finding Our Way Again*. Nashville: Thomas Nelson, 2008.
_____. *New Kind of Christianity, A*. New York: HarperOne, 2010.
Meirs, Nancy. *Ordinary Time*. Boston: Beacon Press, 1993.
Mikva, Rachel, ed. *Broken Tablets: Restoring the Ten Commandments and Ourselves*. Woodstock: Jewish Lights Publishing, 1999.
Miller, Keith. *The Secret Life of the Soul*. Nashville: B & H Publishing, 1997.
Monkhouse, Bob. *Just Say A Few Words*. New York: Virgin Books, 2004.
Monroe, Kelly. *Finding God at Harvard*. Grand Rapids: Zondervan, 1996.
New Interpreter's Bible, The. Nashville: Abingdon Press,

1996.

Norris, Kathleen. *The Cloister Walk.* New York: Riverhead Books, 1996.

Nouwen, Henri. *The Way of the Heart.* New York: Seabury Press, 1981.

Ortberg, John. *If You Want To Walk On Water You've Got To Get Out Of The Boat.* Grand Rapids: Zondervan, 2001.

Paillard, Jean. *In Praise of the Inexpressible.* Peabody, MA.: Henrickson, 2003.

Palmer, Parker. *The Courage to Teach.* San Francisco: Jossey-Bass, 1998.

Peterson, Eugene. *Answering God.* New York: HarperCollins, 1991.

_____. *Message, The.* Colorado Springs: Navpress, 2002.

Powers, John. *And Grace Will Lead Me Home.* New York: McCracken Press, 1994.

Powers, William. *Hamlet's Blackberry.* New York: HarperCollins, 2010.

Raschke, Carl. *The Next Reformation.* Grand Rapids: Baker Academic, 2004.

Rohr, Richard. *The Naked Now.* New York: Crossroad Publishing, 2009.

_____. *Near Occasions of Grace.* Maryknoll, NY.: Orbis Books, 1993.

Rolheiser, Ronald. *Against An Infinite Horizon.* New York: Crossroad Publishing Company, 1995.

Rutledge, Fleming. *Not Ashamed of the Gospel.* Grand Rapids: Eerdmans Publishing, 2007.

Sharma, Robin. *Discover Your Destiny With the Monk Who Sold His Ferrari.* New York: HarperOne, 2006.

Shults, F. LeRon and Sandage, Steven J. *The Faces of*

Forgiveness. Grand Rapids: Baker Academics, 2003.

Shuman, Joel and Roger Owens, eds. *Wendell Berry and Religion.* Lexington: University of Kentucky Press, 2009.

Shurden, Walter, ed. *Proclaiming the Baptist Vision: The Priesthood of All Believers.* Macon: Smyth & Helwys Publishing, 1993.

Sitze, Bob. *Not Trying Too Hard.* Bethesda: The Alban Institute, 2001.

Snyder, Howard. *Decoding the Church.* Grand Rapids: Baker Books, 2002.

Sparks, Susan. *Laugh Your Way to Grace.* Woodstock: Skylight Paths, 2010.

Staub, Dick. *The Culturally Savvy Christian.* San Francisco: John Wiley & Sons, 2007.

Sweet, Leonard. *Gospel According to Starbucks, The.* Colorado Springs, Waterbrook Press, 2007.

_____. *Out of the Question…Into the Mystery.* Colorado Springs: WaterBrook Press, 2004

_____. *Post-Modern Pilgrims.* Nashville: Broadman & Holman, 2000.

_____. *Soul Salsa.* Grand Rapids: Zondervan, 2000.

_____. *Soul Tsunami.* Grand Rapids, Zondervan, 1999.

_____. *The Three Hardest Words in the World to Get Right.* Colorado Springs, Waterbrook Press, 2006.

Taylor, Barbara Brown. *Speaking of Sin.* Cambridge: Cowley Publications, 2000.

Taylor, Brian. *Setting the Gospel Free.* London: SCM Press, 1997.

Thompson, Alden. *Who's Afraid of the Old Testament God?* Gonzalez, FL.: Pacesetters, 2008.

Tippett, Krista. *Speaking of Faith.* New York: Viking Books, 2007.

Tolle, Eckhart. *The Power of Now*. Novato, CA.: New World Library, 2004.
Tuleja, Tad. *Quirky Quotations*. New York: Galahad Books, 1992.
Weaver, C. Douglas. *From Our Christian Heritage*. Macon: Smyth & Helwys, 1997.
Welshons, John. *When Prayers Aren't Answered*. Navato, CA.: New World Library, 2007.
Whale, J. S. *Christian Doctrine*. Cambridge: University Press, 1941.
Willard, Dallas. *The Divine Conspiracy*. New York: HarperCollins, 1998.
Willimon, William. *Peculiar Speech*. Grand Rapids: Eerdmans Publishing, 1992.
Witten, Marsha. *All is Forgiven: The Secular Message in American Protestantism*. Princeton: Princeton University Press, 1995.
Wolpe, David. *Why Faith Matters*. New York: HarperOne, 2008.
Wright, N. T. *After You Believe*. New York: HarperOne, 2010.
_____. *Small Faith, Great God*. Owners Grove, IL.: IVP Books, 2010.
Wuest, Kenneth. *The New Testament: An Expanded Translation*. Grand Rapids, Eerdmans, 1998.
Yancey, Philip. *The Bible Jesus Read*. Grand Rapids: Zondervan, 1999.
_____. *Reaching for the Invisible God*. Grand Rapids: Zondervan, 2001.
_____. *Soul Survivor*. New York: Doubleday, 2003.
_____. *What's So Amazing About Grace?* Grand Rapids: Zondervan, 1997.

About the Author

Ron Higdon, with over fifty years of pastoral experience and ten years of intentional interim ministry, has served churches in Kentucky, Virginia, North Carolina, Texas, and Georgia. He is an intentional interim specialist and a certified church consultant and facilitator. He personally leads study-groups on this book and his previous book, *From Fear to Faith*. He and his wife live in Prospect, Kentucky (a suburb of Louisville) and have two grown sons who live in Atlanta.

His email address is: rbooks5000@aol.com.

www.ingramcontent.com/pod-product-compliance
Lightning Source LLC
Chambersburg PA
CBHW020353170426
43200CB00005B/155